USA ECONOMY FIXING TO CRASH, BRACE FOR IMPACT!

THE MINIMUM WAGE IS STANDING IN THE WAY OF USA SURVIVAL!
Right now the USA has more ability to survive on it's own than any nation on earth. In raw talent, ability, and natural resources the USA is unsurpassed.

The problem with the USA is it has allowed the liberals and their welfare state to get a deadly choke hold on the nation neck and we are being strangled to death. The ultra high taxes and murdering regulations are slowly killing this great nation. It is too late now the USA government no longer has the wisdom or the will to save this great nation in my view.

The ever increasing high taxes and choking regulations will in a couple of years make it impossible for private business to make enough profit to survive. And the economically ignorant general public doesn't have a clue that all government funding originates from the profit of private business.

So, very soon our welfare state ain't

gonna have the funds to save anyone, it is already flat broke and you can juggle the books and run schemes but only so long. As of now the people themselves are the only thing that can save the great USA.

They can still save the great USA by buying, selling, and maybe even bartering with each other to feed themselves and survive, after all people traded and bartered for thousands of years before money was invented.

In fact the American Indian survived for centuries and never had a currency. To survive sometimes you gotta do what you gotta do. One must have food, shelter, and warmth to survive, then every thing else is gravy when times get hard enough.

Going this route hopefully the government can still tax enough to maintain security if nothing else, at this stages this is the wisest course to take. Otherwise if we keep trying to save the welfare state I guarantee you we will end up with a dictator or some form of authoritarian rule, and if that happens 100 million starving to death will be a low figure in my view.

There is no doubt in my mind if allowed to the people will take the bull by the horns and do whatever it take to survive. The people can and will save the great USA but there is a problem, as it is they can't, even it being the last chance and hope for USA survival.

You see, the "Minimum wage is standing right dab in the middle of the way and if it is not ripped up by the root and completely eliminated it is over for the great USA, we will be totally doomed. I have pounded and pounded this fact to no end all to no avail everyone seems to think I'm crazy.

But, where there is a will there is always a way and I still have hope. So, as long as there is still breath in my body I will be pounding for the elimination of the minimum wage. Just maybe enough people will wake up before it is too late.

Thank you God for my life, health, and strength, I am truly blessed and have so much to live for, thank you, thank you, thank you...
SIRMANS LOG: 14 SEPTEMBER 2012, 1905 HOURS

WELL, I GUESS I FINALLY LOST MY COTTON PICKING MIND.
I am only one man, a pitiful looking little neurotic handicap armed only with a pen going up against this awesome almighty omnipotent welfare state. It is just like the classic battle of David going up against Goliath armed only with a slingshot.

I think in about four years the socialist/liberal news media is going to be the most surprised of all. That is because they are the first ones that must go when a dictator or an authoritarian government starts consolidating power.

USA ECONOMY FIXING TO CRASH, BRACE FOR IMPACT!

Like I've said before I believe the economy is going to totally collapse within four years. That being the case I think the take over will start with martial law, and then a dictator or some type of authoritarian regime will emerge.

The only thing that is going to save the America economy from a totally collapse is the complete elimination of the minimum wage, period, nothing else can save us. Mainly because the welfare state has destroyed any backup or safely valve to survive on likes a strong nuclear and extended family system.

The things that allowed civilization to survive for over 5,000 years like a strong nuclear and extended family system, strong moral and family values, and adequate emergency backup bartering capacity with many, many small farmers and home gardeners are all almost nonexistent.

We have almost no means of surviving when the economy totally collapses.

And that is a fact that the liberals are too shallow to ever see until people starts starving by the millions. It is completely get rid of the minimum wage or back to the Stone Age, there is no other option.

I'm no fool I know today's politicians will never totally eliminate the minimum wage, still, I must never stop pounding and pounding away because it is my destiny and duty to keep sounding the distress call, come hell or high waters. God save America.
SIRMANS LOG: 12 SEPTEMBER 2012, 2049 HOURS

AGAIN, THE MINIMUM wage MUST BE RIPPED UP BY THE ROOT AND COMPLETELY ELIMINATED.
I know a lot of people don't understand my thinking and writing, but, I'm not just out here free wheeling it there is a method to my insanity or wisdom that guides me.

So, let me shine some light on what

guides me. The reason I know without a shadow of a doubt that I am right and in time will be vindicated is because my thinking is in line with nature's supreme law of "Natural selection."

A society must have government for the protection of the whole society, but, pertaining to the economy government involvement and force is the worst thing you can have. That is because force flies into the face of nature's supreme law of "Natural selection."

The law of "Natural selection" is what controls everything and all existence, and it is based on a survival need. If there is no survival need for it, any and everything starts ceasing to exist. The old saying is really true, "If you don't use it you lose it."

So, when government forces a "Minimum wage" on the people the ability to hire people at any cost starts ceasing to exist. Even a giant mighty oak tree didn't start big but instead started from a wee little acorn.

The "Minimum wage" must be ripped up by the root and completely eliminated if the USA and western civilization is to have any chance of survival. Otherwise, according to nature's supreme law of "Natural selection" it will be impossible for the USA to survive as 57 states, every special interest group and faction in the nation will soon be at each others throat.

There will be no way of avoiding it, back to the Stone Age will be our destination. I know that around 99.9 percent of the American people think I'm insane for wanting to completely get rid of the minimum wage, still that don't prove me wrong.

God has blessed me with this great super natural wisdom for a reason. No matter how handicapped or seemingly unqualified I may be the distress call must be sounded and go forth regardless, it is my destiny and it is bigger than my well being or survival.

This whole thing is like the classic battle of good versus evil. There are some who think my way of thinking represents evil by wanting to set things back to when many didn't have certain rights. But, I'm not about taking away anyone's rights I am strictly against anything of the sort.

What I am about is saving human beings and many of the old values is what allowed civilization to survive for over 5,000 years. The nuclear family, good moral values, and adequate bartering capacity are a must, and without them no society can survive for very long, period.

Today in the USA every one of those three values is in almost total ruins. I have no bitterness towards anyone; I know I can see much more than the average person in term of survival.

An example is like many people that have been severely injured or had something bad happen to them, but

later said they was glad it happened because it opened their eyes, and they can now see things that was always right before their eyes.
SIRMANS LOG: 8 SEPTEMBER 2012, 1026 HOURS

CAN GENERAL MOTORS WITHSTAND THE TEST OF TIME?
Folks, I try to leave certain things alone, but I just couldn't hold my tongue any longer or I was going to pop if I didn't vent. What I am talking about is all of this bragging by the shallow minded liberals about saving general motors.

Well, I for one have a different opinion about that matter. In my view liberals just simply doesn't have the depth to understand democracy or the free market, period. Our liberal created welfare state is what has created all these shallow minded liberals that are coming out of the woodworks armed with unsound judgment.

The liberals have not saved general motors what they really have done is made it another big government dependent. The very basics of understanding life, growth, and survival, or just existence itself are to know that you have to get rid of rot, decay, and inefficiency.

You just simply can't have progress, growth, and long term success without allowing failure. What government has actually done to general motors is create another burden on the American tax payers. And from now on it will always be a burden because its management will never make the hard decisions to get rid of enough rot, decay, and inefficiency to become totally independent and profitable.

Sure, it is propped up now, but this government is broke and will soon be going under, then what? This nation has bankruptcy laws which mean general motors would have survived, but leaner and meaner, I think saving the unions and keeping liberal voters happy definitely was a factor. But, instead we have a wobbly kneed colossal big government dependent for life.

In closing, I'm just one self-made neurotic writer with an opinion, what the hell do I know?
SIRMANS LOG: 6 SEPTEMBER 2012, 2337 HOURS

WHAT DO AFRICANS AMERICANS AND WOMEN HAVE IN COMMON?

What do African Americans and women have in common; they both have a very high dependency mentality. This is not intended to put these two demographics down in any way; this is to try to understand the why of this phenomenon.

Plus, I don't think this is necessarily a bad thing, it allowed African Americans as a race to survive in a hostile environment right out of slavery. But, this is a new day and it is time for African Americans as a race to think as individuals and be more responsible for their own survival.

When are Africans Americans on a wide scale going to provide more of their own businesses to provide jobs and do more of the hiring of their own people, cry me a river? I am retired now, but over the years I have hired people and provided jobs.

On a mass scale what the hell survival need can a poor black man offer a woman when uncle sugar is her Great white father provider, you tell me. To act responsible there must be a survival need to be responsible according to nature's supreme law of "Natural selection."

The welfare state has just about taken all responsibility away from the poor black man in the African American community, and the rest of the nation will soon follow suit. So, how can you expect someone to be responsible when they have never been conditioned to be responsible, you can't logically? I totally blame the shallow minded liberals for this situation.

As a writer I am only trying to get at the facts and wade through all of the myths and emotionalism. I'm one that believes that almost nothing about life is innate; it is all learned in some way. I believe a new born baby's brain starts off as a clean slate.

So, there must be a logical reason why 90 percent plus African Americans as a group always vote for one political party. It is like the unbreakable bond between a mother and child. In my books and writings I go deep into the reasons why African Americans think the way they do.

But, for now I will move on to the political reality of dealing with the said two demographics groups. If conservatives and republicans are thinking about winning these two groups over with reason, forget it, it ain't gonna happen. There is an emotional bond here with the Democratic Party that can't be broken with no amount of reasoning.

These two groups see the Democratic Party like a child sees its parents. It is all about dependency versus independency. Dependency is the nesting syndrome, and the only way to break the nesting syndrome is to kick the dependent out of the nest, that is what the mother eagle does.

But, for African Americans, mentally we are still in the nest and will stay there as long as we have a welfare state. And the really sad part is the welfare state has almost totally destroyed the African American culture and nuclear family and is fast working on the entire nation.

And another thing, the poverty pimps are making sure that African Americans never leave the safety of the nest. They guarantee that African Americans won't ever be able to jettison their dependency slave mentality.

African Americans still mentally see the master's beer as colder and if given a choice won't automatically support his look alike brothers and sisters in business or otherwise.

The African American elite won't create zones in and around an all African American neighborhood to live but instead get as far away as they can afford.

Sure, the excuse now is crime is the big problem but I don't buy that for one second as the only reason, because the movie "A raising in the sun" showed escaping from black neighborhoods long before the welfare state kicked the black man out of the home to create all of this crime.

I see a culture problem here, but the poverty pimps are still fighting both tooth and nails to keep African Americans in the nest as helpless victims, instead of taking more responsibility for our own survival come hell of high waters.

As a race we owned and controlled far more before the welfare state came along and destroyed the black community. My God what a sad situation, still, I wish all people goodwill including the good intention poverty pimps.

It is the welfare state that has created all of these dependents and if they haven't reached a majority yet it is only a matter of time before they do and send us all back to the Stone Age.

I think we still have a majority in hard working tax payers and independents that will give conservatives and republicans a political Trifecta in November but just barely, on one condition.

That one condition is the republicans must pound and pound to no end low taxes, more jobs, and strong national defense. Otherwise, Lord knows I hope I'm wrong, but I just don't believe the republicans can win it otherwise.

Myself, I am a conservative at heart but in practice I'm a realist.
SIRMANS LOG: 31 AUGUST 2012, 1303 HOURS

CURRENT EVENTS:
WHY CRUCIFY ONE FOR A BAD CHOICE OF WORDS?
This abortion flap going around that is supposed to be so outrageous is only a modern thing. Until within the last one hundred years an unborn child conceived through rape was almost never killed.

In fact some believe that the child itself acts as a healing process from a horrible traumatic event. Back then the racial element was the only thing that guaranteed the killing of the unborn child of the rape victim in some cases.

So, in my opinion why should a poor choice of words create all of this ado about something the moral bankrupted liberals would like to exploit? And all liberals are not democrats. This is the sort of thing that can end up biting the self-righteous.

What is freedom if a man can't defend the unborn; we have no future if no

one defends the unborn. It's no wonder social security is going under we have killed off a whole generation of payers.
SIRMANS LOG: 21 AUGUST 2012, 0150 HOURS

FAR TOO MANY AMERICANS ARE JUST PLAIN ECONOMICALLY IGNORANT! Economically speaking "What belongs to everyone belongs to no one," in theory, maybe not, but, in actually practice it's definitely true.

Okay, this idea that the government did it, that the roads, bridges, and infrastructure provided the means or the individual couldn't have done it is shallow negative thinking in my view, but many liberals think that way.

That type of thinking places the cart before the horse. Government is a necessary parasite that every society must have to provide internal and external protection. In a free society government can't sustain itself or produce a profit, it survives only on what it takes in the form of profit from what always originates from some form of private business transaction, period.

Sure, the government got the roads, bridges, and infrastructure, but, where the hell you think government got the seized money from to do that? Not that I disagree, but it got the money out of the profit of many, many struggling small businesses.

All of this anti-business propaganda is just plain economic ignorance.
They have no idea what made America the greatest and wealthiest nation in the history of mankind.

Without the millions upon millions of small private businesses out there making a profit there will be no profit for the government to take to provide anything for anyone, period.

Lord have mercy on our great nation, with all of this negative anti-business propaganda thinking out there we are going to need it.

USA ECONOMY FIXING TO CRASH, BRACE FOR IMPACT!

SIRMANS LOG: 20 AUGUST 2012, 1201 HOURS

IF THE REPUBLICAN DOESN'T WIN A POLITICAL TRIFECTA IN NOVEMBER IT WILL BE THEIR OWN FAULT!
I have pounded it to where I am almost blue in the face; conservatives limit your message to around three things. Sure, you respond to any and everything then its I stands by my earlier statement.

I know staying with so few things will bore the hell out of most people
but that is what you want, that is proof they are not forgetting what you stand for.

The simple minded and many others will succumb to the course of least resistance and grab the democrat goodies that is why the default vote Almost always goes to the democrats. And unless a conservative stand for lower taxes, more jobs, and strong national defense the default vote Will carry the day in the general election most of the time.

In my view the problem with the republicans is they are out there attacking for blood and is acting and reacting all over the map and no one truly knows what they stand for. To hell with the other guy, the people want to know what about you, what are you gonna do, can I trust and depend on you.

The hard working independents and majority tax paying voters will never desert one who pounds to no end lower taxes, more jobs, and strong national defense. Yet, somewhere in the polling it got republicans running away from the three things I advocate especially lower taxes.

I say to hell with all of this polling go with your gut sometime, people want someone who is willing to go down with what they themselves believe in and what is right for America.

I will tell you now if you are afraid to pound away on lower taxes your

chance of winning in November are going to be slim to none and that is nobodies fault but your own.
SIRMANS LOG: 14 AUGUST 2012, 0852 HOURS

THE REPUBLICANS WILL WIN IN NOVEMBER 2012, BUT, I BELIEVE THEY TOO WILL FAIL, TOO!
Well, we now know who the republican vice presidential candidate will be and my prediction was wrong. Obviously there is going to be a new team after November 2012, but, in my view the republicans will at least buy a little more time before the USA and world economy collapses. Otherwise, to keep the same team we go dictatorship or some other authoritarian rule right away because I believe the economy will totally collapse within three years.

The sad fact is THE WELFARE STATE can't be saved and anyone that thinks it can is in denial. I can dissect an economy as well as anyone and I'm telling you the days of the welfare state is over we are now living on borrowed time.

The republicans just as the democrats are dead set on saving the welfare state but I'm telling you the republicans will fail even worse than the dems simply because they think they can cut the growth of government, wrong.

It is impossible to reduce the growth of government in this welfare state because there are too many social programs that will kick in and increase the dole side of government, thereby growing government in a reverse negative way. There is no need to add more details they can be found farther down in my writing.

All I will say at this time is we must start somewhere to prevent going back to the Stone Age. The first thing that must be done or nothing else matters anyway because holding on to the welfare state leads only back to the Stone Age.

The complete elimination of the

minimum wage must be done now or it will be impossible for the USA government to survive, that is a fact, there is not a doubt in my super mind about that. You don't have to believe me just keep on living; the minimum wage must go, one way or another if we are to have any chance of survival as a nation.

I pound and pound this fact and still no one wants to hear it but we all will sooner than we think. The elimination of the minimum wage will allow the American people to save themselves because soon the government is not going to have the money to do so.

The government doesn't generate any profit it is a necessary parasite and every penny it takes in comes from some form of private business profit. And in this anti-business atmosphere the shallow minded liberals are trying to make it impossible for a business to make a profit.

The liberal and masses of economically ignorant government dependents are

biting the hand that feed them and the really sad part is they don't have a clue absent the bias predominant socialist/liberal news media. God I ask in your name, save the only home I know.
SIRMANS LOG: 12 AUGUST 2012, 0203 HOURS
PS: All solutions on how to save the USA economy and western civilization can be found farther down in my writing.

WHO WILL BE THE 2012 REPUBLICAN VICE PRESIDENTIAL CANDIDATE? Only the republican presidential candidate himself, his wife, and just maybe a very few trusted confidants knows. Still, that doesn't stop almost everyone from the political experts to the man on the streets from guessing who it will be. I decided to join the crowd and participate in the guessing game.

With nothing more to go on but my own gut feelings I'm taking a shot in the dark and predicting the republican

vice presidential candidate will be Rick Santorum. There will be no surprises there; I think the governor is a very, very cautious man.
SIRMANS LOG: 5 AUGUST 2012, 0928 HOURS

ARE REPUBLICANS AFRAID TO PROMOTE LOWER TAXES?
Folks, I am a self-made writer and a screwed up neurotic one at that.
But, one thing I am not is a phony hypocrite. I may not be a man of extra strong physical courage and feel overall I am too passive. Still, I think I am a man of conviction and I try to do my best in spite of my handicaps.

I said all of that to try to make a point, it is no wonder the survival of our freedom is under attack. I feel we may lose our freedom because fewer and fewer people are willing to standby their true convictions.
Every politician seems to be putting a finger up into the wind by means of political polling.

The republicans had a TRIFECTA in the bag, but, I feel they stand a good chance of losing now simply because they are too afraid to stand up to their convictions. Instead they are putting all of their faith in all of this extreme polling; I hope they are right for the sake of the country and our freedom.

I really don't have a favorite political party my only concern is who will best hold on to our dwindling supply of freedom. Even if the republicans do win the TRIFECTA it will only allow a little more time before nature's supreme law of "Natural selection" lowers the boom.

The republicans don't need to give out a lot of details all they need to do is just pound and pound to no end lower taxes, more jobs, and strong national defense and nothing else. But, I believe they are afraid to pound lower taxes, and what I say to that is when the majority of Americans don't want lower taxes the country is no long worth saving anyway.

If that is the case there soon won't be any freedom left to save. We will be a bankrupted welfare state headed back to the Stone Age. No matter what our beliefs are we all are Americans, you don't have to agree with anything I write, but thank God I still have the freedom to say the things I write.
SIRMANS LOG: 30 JULY 2012, 1219 HOURS

IS THE PENN STATE SLATE WIPED CLEAN ENOUGH?
As a writer with extreme perspective and supernatural wisdom sometimes I feel a need to stop in my tracks and just vent. As I look at world civilization and see where it is today I believe it was the dominant western civilization that lead us here.

But, ever since the "New deal" and the birth of the welfare state we have lost our way. I know the great scholars and thinkers have come up with all kinds of reasons of the why of the decline.

But, as a creative super deep original

thinker I have zeroed in on the lack of teaching the Christian faith as a big factor. And to focus in on even a more precise point which is our loss of the Power of forgiveness. Culture wise it is a fact that unforgiveness stops growth and progress in its track and a slow primitive regression backward begins.

Sure, there is an exception to every thing in life but as a rule the most caring and forgiving people are those that have faced the most hardships and struggles. The Penn State case prompted me to write this article. All I ask is where does individual accountability end?

No one can control what another person may do. Do we really want to go all the way back to the seventh generation like in the Old Testament to make sure the slate is clean? It may come to that insanity.
SIRMANS LOG: 23 JULY 2012, 1229 HOURS

A CONSERVATIVE WILL ALMOST

ALWAYS LOSE THE GENERAL ELECTION BY CONSTANTLY ATTACKING!
Unless one has deep wisdom and perspective they won't understand why I'm so against all of this attacking. It is simply because it is a loser's strategy.

Today's voter has a short attention span and need to be constantly reminded of who you are and what you stand for. Sure, attacking the other guy tears him down, but that doesn't remind quick forgetting independents and the majority what you stand for.

Everyone already knows the sugar daddy/momma liberal is going to tax and spend and give away the store even when we can't afford it, especially women and African Americans already know this, they just don't care.

It is like the warnings on a pack of cigarettes and all of the warnings against big juicy high fat burgers, etc.

people already know the danger and choose high risk living, so preaching fire and brimstone on how bad someone or something is may work against a conservative but very little against a sugar daddy liberal giving out goodies. As long as the goodies keep coming they will say "I don't care if the canidate looks like ET as long he is nice to me."

Knowing better we all has a weakness to take the course of lease resistance and grab the goodies, but if a mature conservative step up and promise lower taxes, more jobs, and strong national defense he will win with the independents and majority tax paying public.

I'm telling you, in the general election you don't normally beat a liberal by constantly attacking, Reagan didn't go that route nor did "W." Attacking in itself distracts from who you are and what you stand for, and in the final analysis that is the reason people vote, the individual
sometimes has little to do with it.

I would but there is no way in hell 90 percent plus African Americans would vote for Herman Cain. He would be the best friend we ever had but there is an indelible stamp on too many out there that says his way of thinking is the enemy. Sure, some people will vote for you simply because they hate the other guy so much, but in most cases it is going to take a lot more than that to win.

So, those are the facts, it is what it is. It is what you are going to do that really matters and if conservatives are not going to stress lower taxes, more jobs, and strong national defense I don't believe we will get the trifecta in November. I certainly hope I'm wrong on this.
SIRMANS LOG: 18 JULY 2012, 1440 HOURS

"NEVER LET THEM SEE YOU SWEAT"
Conservatives stay the course, stay the course the socialist/liberal
news media shark feeding frenzy is a

sign of desperation to try to break your pounding grip of low taxes, more jobs, and strong national defense only for the guaranteed TRIFECTA win in November.

If you let them break your death grip now we lose the TRIFECTA win it's just that simple. People got eyes and ears and independents and the majority will never vote against one that relentlessly pounds low taxes, more jobs, and strong national defense only unless the socialist/liberal news media breaks your death grip.

Just keep pounding those three priorities to no end because that is your armor and no minds will change, except around forty percent who will never vote for a conservative anyway. "Never let them see you sweat" just keep pounding; pounding and pounding, freedom in America depends on it.

They are going to throw everything at you including the kitchen sink if you are a conservative or have any

conservative's leanings, but just keep pounding the said priorities and they will never turn the independents against you.
SIRMANS LOG: 17 JULY 2012, 2101 HOURS

IT'S OVER FOLKS; I DON'T SEE ANYTHING BREAKING THE DEATH GRIP CONSERVATIVES HOLD.
It is just a matter of time before all of the flailing has to peter out. Unless the pit bull like ceaseless pounding of low taxes, more jobs, and strong national defense eases up it is definitely over.

However, conservatives never ease up or take anything for granted because it in never official over until the last vote is counted. The TRIFECTA super prize win is unofficial now a done deal, hurry up 3 November.

Let them flail away and holler all they want to because nothing short of easing up on the low taxes, more jobs, and strong national defense pounding can deny conservatives the

USA ECONOMY FIXING TO CRASH, BRACE FOR IMPACT!

big TRIFECTA in November.
SIRMANS LOG: 15 JULY 2012, 1538 HOURS

CONSERVATIVES NOW HAVE A DEATH GRIP ON A BIG TRIFECTA WIN IN NOVEMBER!
I'm hearing people say attack back, which is the normal thing to do, but that is what the attack dog socialist/liberal news media want you to do so you will then be in their brier patch and people will forget what the hell you stand for, and then they can rip you apart with a thousand cuts.

I say to the conservatives you now have the death grip just hold on like a pit bull by keep pounding nonstop low taxes, more jobs, and strong national defense. You see the proof that it is working by them flailing away with all kinds of lies and extremes like crazy trying to break your death grip on the TRIFECTA win in November.

Their insane flailing is only preaching

to their own choir, the independents and majority will never abandon one who pounds endlessly low taxes, more jobs, and strong national defense. Discipline, discipline, no matter what, just keep pounding the said priorities and get the TRIFECTA win in November. Glory be to God.
SIRMANS LOG: 13 JULY 2012, 2250 HOURS

I BELIEVE CONSERVATIVES HAS A SLIM TO NONE CHANCE OF WINNING THE BIG TRIFECTA IN NOVEMBER WITHOUT ADHERING TO MY ADVICE! This is my advice to all conservatives or anyone with conservatives leaning; never stray from only three things, low taxes, more jobs, and strong national defense.

Sure, make just one statement on current events or what ever but then revert back to the three said priorities, period. The attack dog predominate socialist/liberal news media don't like you and is going to
do everything in their power to defeat

you. That said, as a rule the
general public tends to be simple
minded with short memories.

That means to win the big TRIFECTA
conservatives must keep it simple
with not more than the three priorities,
low taxes, more jobs, and strong
national defense only. Sure, doing that
will bore the hell out of most people,
but that is what you want up until the
election that will be proof that they
won't forget what you stand for.

Otherwise, off to the side stirring up
controversial and everything else
the independents and others attention
span won't remember what the
hell you stand for, then the liberal news
media will rip you apart. No
matter what the liberal news media
propaganda attack machine says
the independents and winning majority
will remain faithful and loyal if
you never depart from the three said
priorities, they are your armor.

I'm telling every conservative or
anyone with conservative leaning if

USA ECONOMY FIXING TO CRASH, BRACE FOR IMPACT!

you don't take my advice we have a slim to none chance of winning the big TRIFECTA in November. That is just the way it is. There are no absolute guarantees in life the most anyone can do is create the best conditions to win.

The liberal news media propaganda attack machine in my view is the biggest obstacle standing between a big TRIFECTA conservative win for the conservatives in November. All they know is to attack, attack, and attack, and it is futile to try to defend against their every barrage without armor.

The three said priorities is your armor only if you bore the hell out of people by sticking only with them. Sticking with them conservatives win, veering off them then the liberal news media propaganda attack machine will rip you apart and defeat you.

God I ask in your name save our great nation.
SIRMANS LOG: 12 JULY 2012, 1227

HOURS

WHAT IS IT ABOUT THE MINIMUM WAGE THAT PEOPLE CAN'T UNDERSTAND?
Cutting the minimum wage is cold, wrong and a mistake, doing that will only aggravate and increase poor people's misery. No one has ever read or heard me encourage lowering the minimum wage, if you thought you did you weren't listening.

I have been drum beating it until I'm almost blue in the face to "Get rid of the minimum wage that is a world of difference from lowering the minimum wage. I am talking about eliminating the minimum wage entirely, period. That is the only things that would bring back some sanity to our economy, and is the only thing that will save the USA with freedom intact.

Otherwise, welfare states worldwide will become dictatorships or some other form of authoritarian rule within five years just to keep order. What people that lack perspective and a basic understanding of economics fail to realize is it is not the amount of money that matters; it is the buying power that truly counts.

Eliminating the minimum wage for the whole nation would shift the economy into a natural balance where money would count for something, or there would be no way to prevent bartering. The minimum wage is what allowed the welfare state a foot in the door, now the welfare state beast rules the roost.

A free market place economy is bases on the fact that any one can pay as much or less as he sees fit for a job so long as no one is forced to accept it, or even pay the help with commodities if no force is applied. Sure, what I just said was to the extreme, but, I am all about survival, and with the condition the USA is in financial, nothing should be ruled out.

In my humble opinion the only thing

stopping the USA from becoming a dictatorship right now is the second amendment. However, after November all of that could drastically change, I think the hidden priority agenda will be to use some type of UN treaty to trump the second amendment and override the second amendment once and for all. That is my analysis.

The liberals are just waiting on their chance to pounce. I ask in your name, God save freedom in America. SIRMANS LOG: 10 JULY 2012, 1447 HOURS

NEGATIVE ADS WORK, SURE, WITH IGNORANT AND UNINFORMED PEOPLE, BUT NOT WITH ME.
I'm one that has never bought into this idea that negative ads always work. Sure, they work with the ignorant and uninformed but not everyone fits that description.

I hold to the rule that if you are a good and decent person and makes sure people know what you stand for then good and decent people will support you. In politics I think the dumbest thing one can do is exercise in futility by trying to defend against every bad or incorrect charge directed against you. At worst even if they brand you a SOB, what else is new, like Nixon said, sure, he is a SOB but he is our SOB.

As long as the conservatives keep pounding low taxes, creating more jobs, and strong national defense and nothing else the independents and vast majority won't care what the bias socialist/liberal news media propaganda attack machine brands you. And they will prove it by saying he is our SOB with their vote.

But, if the conservatives get side tracked into shouting matches of he said she said and every other kind of juicy fodder it will be just what the doctor ordered for the liberal propaganda machine. Then with phony polls and every other kind of distortion one can imaging the

liberal propaganda attack machine will rip you to threads and defeat you. Staying with the three said things is your armor, don't abandon them.
SIRMANS LOG: 4 JULY 2012, 1759 HOURS

GET OVER IT CONSERVATIVES OBAMACARE IS NOW THE LAW OF THE LAND AND THAT IS A FACT!
About this new Supreme Court ruling on Obamacare, I think some conservatives just ought to get over it, period. They should realize what the liberals have always known that the constitution means only what five people say it means.

From a political point of view you control the court with the legislative process by controlling who get on it, not by ranting on and on over spilled milk. Why do you think the die hard liberals always fight to the last man/woman over who gets on the court, wake up and wise up conservatives, it is all about control,

not ranting.
SIRMANS LOG: 4 JULY 2012, 1045 HOURS

A CONSERVATIVE ROYAL FLUSH WINNING HAND. NEW INJECTION ADD-ON #2
In my view this whole Supreme Court ruling is actually a God send to conservatives. If conservative can't get an overwhelming trifecta win out of this they never will. With this ruling conservatives is now holding a royal flush sure winner going into the November election.

However, the problem is the conservatives don't know what to do even if they do win the big trifecta prize. The welfare state needs to be dismantled and taken down but they don't have the will or guts to take on that issue.

The welfare state beast without a doubt is going to soon collapse eating us all one by one alive in the process, so, where is the wisdom in failing to take down this beast when you have the power in your hands to do so.

I doubt there will be any real changes if the conservatives win big, I think they will just try to feed the beast a lot less by cutting back on everything, which will end up even worse than what the liberals did.

The reason why is we have a complete welfare state and when you start cutting back all that does is increase the dole population, which is a no, no. There is simply no way out except using my "Any nation emergency survival plan" which you will find further down in my writing.
SIRMANS LOG: 2 JULY 2012, 2308 HOURS

NEW INJECTION: ADD-ON
In hind sight I think the court probably did do the wisest thing. Otherwise the whole liberal establishment would be up in arms
accusing the court of someone who

takes candy from a baby.

To save freedom in America it is going to take a miracle anyway, we are too far gone. The liberal news media propaganda machine has brain washed far too many people, that the government owes them a living.
I'm telling you there are no free rides in nature, one way or another someone always pays.

The liberal news media propaganda machine has dumbed down the population to the point now that the dead beats and non-producer are attacking the producers and the people that makes this country work,
which is political suicide. "The inmates are now beginning to take over the asylum."

It is all starting to come to a head and the election in November is only how fast we lose our freedom. If the democratic win the saving freedom battle is totally lost and if the republicans win it will only slow the process down, but at least allow more time for a possible miracle.

Either way it is now time for Katie to bar the door. Forty percent are going to vote democratic no matter what and forty percent are going to vote republican no matter what, but, now I believe the lions share of the 20 percent independent swing vote is going republican because of Obamacare.

Freedom of the individual is on trial and without a miracle I don't see any hope of it surviving. I have thrown out a lifeline for the only way out but so far no one wants to take my bitter medicine. I have offered my bitter medicine throughout my writing many times before with no takers, but I will briefly outline it again.

Our welfare state provider government is the root problem; it has reached a tax raising saturation point and can't be saved. This is what must be done to save the USA and welfare states world wide to prevent them from becoming dictatorships or some other form of authoritarian rule.

With no exception the minimum wage must be eliminated first and now, not tomorrow or when we get around to it. Next, government spending must be separated from the free market national economy now, not later. This separation can only be done by government establishing its own commissaries, housing, and clinics with the use of tokens or script.

This can be done almost overnight with so many empty vacant building in American cities. Excluding government employees government must never give anyone free unearned money to spend in the national free market economy that act alone is like incest it pollutes and contaminates the free market with consumer inflation.

It is like eating your seed corn or drinking your priming water, that is the main thing that has acted like a cancer that have ate up welfare states from the inside out worldwide. Sure, government has a duty as a last resort to help the poor and disadvantage but never with cash handouts that will contaminate and destroy the national free market economy.

Government must operate it own commissaries, housing, and clinics with the use of tokens or script to keep it's spending separate and not destroy the national economy. There is no if's and's, or but's about it, if my solution is not accepted the welfare states worldwide will end up as dictatorships or some other form of authoritarian rule.

Freedom cannot and will not survive without most of its people disciplined with a sense of responsibility and accountability, period. The USA is almost there at the point of no return, far too many people thinks the government owes them a living with free Medicare. That is like asking doctors and health care workers to be slaves and give you free

Medicare.

The welfare state has all but completely destroyed our once strong nuclear and extended family system, our use to be strong religious and moral way of life, and our former adequate emergency backup bartering capacity with many small farmers and home gardeners, in case the economy collapsed.

Now, we have nothing in terms of raw survival when this bloated welfare state collapses which could happen any day now. When the USA and welfare states world wide starts collapsing which could happen overnight and people get hungry only an iron fist can maintain order. And I'm not for sure even that will save civilization from ending back in the Stone Age.

Yet, they say I'm crazy and off my rocker, so be it as long as I can convince just one thick scull how dire our situation is. I'll say it like this, in the final analysis it is get rid of the welfare states or accept our fate and perish.

If we keep trying to save the welfare state nothing is going to save freedom and free enterprise, and I would bet my life on that if it would make a difference.
SIRMANS LOG: 1 JULY 2012, 1955 HOURS. NEW INJECTION END

I'm fixing to say something I shouldn't say and I don't know why I'm saying it but knowing me I'm going to say it anyway. I have said many times throughout my writing that "The Lord works in mysterious ways."

Well, no one disagrees more of what the Chief Justice did than me, it just doesn't make sense in my view. I have come to a conclusion that this is a case of divine intervention and a display of the power of destiny. Anyone with wisdom and perspective knows this is an earth shaking political game changer.

This is a conservative winning hand

that even an idiot can't screw up. Still, "Nothing is written in stone, and never count your chicken before they hatch."
SIRMANS LOG: 20 JUNE 2012, 2150 HOURS

CONFIRMING OBAMACARE MAY BE THE STRAW THAT BROKE THE CAMELS BACK! WOW! OMG! Sold, sold, and sold by the biggest bait and switch sale wrap-up of the century. "My congrats to the Lib's."

As one who loves freedom of the individual I will be the first to disagree with the Supreme Court confirming OBAMACARE. However, why fret folks, because in the grand scheme of things the Supreme Court decision only speeds up the demise of our welfare state.

It is obvious the USA is going to go the failed socialist course of Western Europe, duh. In my view this is a sad day for freedom loving Americans. To make it simple where even an idiot can understand, the days of the welfare state are over, we are broke, no money, can't pay, empty pockets, what about no money people can't seem understand, duh.

Financial wise the welfare state cannot and will not survive, period. In a way this confirming OBAMACARE may be a blessing in disguise. The working people who pay the bills and make this country work may finally wake up and vote in only genuine conservative or face losing this great land of the free and home of the brave.

Far too many people think the nation owe them a living from years of the liberal news media propaganda. You can't get blood out of a turnip simply because there is none there; it is the same with OBAMACARE there is no money there to pay for it which is promoting false hope to the people.

The USA government is already borrowing forty cents of every dollar it spends. And surely this big

OBAMACARE add-on is going to be the straw that broke the camel's back. May God have mercy on the USA after this extreme lack of sound judgment by people in high places?

God bless these leaders I'm sure they did what they though what was best for the country, it is not perfect, still it is our system and I support it one hundred percent without a doubt. God bless America.
SIRMANS LOG: 28 JUNE 2012, 1208 HOURS

"We have a republic if we can keep it," that is truer today than it was over 200 years ago.

A BAD MARRIAGE!
I keep hearing market, market, and market to no end, and I'm sick and tired of it. That is the biggest problem with the USA and welfare states worldwide. The governments of local, state, and federal need to get the hell out of the stock market and the stock market need to get the hell

out of the government.

They are two different things and don't mix. All government spending especially on an individual basis must be kept separated from the free market place economy, period, or else.
SIRMANS LOG: 20 JUNE 2012, 2024 HOURS

A MOMENT OF THINKING OUT LOUD!
I am paraphrasing, "There goes the dreamer, lets slay him and then see what happens to his dream. The waves of sin are a slow death to me."
SIRMANS LOG: 18 JUNE 2012, 0013 HOURS

MY MINIMUM WAGE CRUSADE
One way or another the minimum wage is going to be completely eliminated. It boils down to how it gets done. At some point soon nature's Supreme law of "Natural selection" is going to do it for the USA and all welfare states world wide unless we act first.

Ever since the "New deal" we have let the liberals call the tune and give away the store now we have to pay the piper in blood, sweat, and tears, and even that may not be enough to save our nation.

There is no escaping our lack of judgment; it is a law of nature, there are no free rides. However, if the USA and the welfare states world wide go ahead and completely eliminate the minimum wage first modern civilization may be saved.

Otherwise, if nature's supreme law of "Natural selection" has to lower the boom then once the dominoes starts falling it may mean all the way back to the Stone Age.

God, I ask in your name stay your hand!
SIRMANS LOG: 12 JUNE 2012, 1559 HOURS

SOME SOUL FOOD FOR THOUGHT

INJECTION, HERE.
Come on folks, I believe a new team will be going in next year. "Big deal! You are just one unknown self-made writer with an opinion. Get lost." However, I don't think I am alone on thinking this, I think the lib's want to change horses in midstream but don't know how without losing their 90 percent plus African American monopoly vote forever. But, find a way to blame it on the republicans, problem solved.

Now, chew on that for a while. I'm a creative writer folks, this is just food for though and the wild imagination of my deep, deep thinking. God save our great nation.
SIRMANS LOG: 8 JUNE 2012, 1930 HOURS

"ANY NATION EMERGENCY SURVIVAL PLAN" BY FREDDIE L. SIRMANS, SR.
Folks, I am a self-made writer and I tell it as I see it, straight raw no chaser, right or wrong, believe it or not, take it or leave it is what you

get from me.

Never mind the experts and learned economist, I Freddie L. Sirmans, Sr. with my great supernatural wisdom is offering my "Any nation emergency survival plan." Its coming folks, a totally economic collapse, and I am offering my plan free to prevent total chaos that may lead back to the Stone Age.

No, I haven't lost my mind I have been writing basically the same thing for over twenty years, now. Here is the first thing that should be done now even before nature's supreme law of "Natural selection" lowers the boom.

Any nation that expects to survive when the boom is lowered and the domino's starts falling best take heed and act now because the whole thing may be like a fast moving tree top wild fire. Number one, the USA and all of the welfare state must completely get rid of the "Minimum wage" now, not tomorrow or when you get around to it.

That would set free the free market place where it would function naturally like it is supposed to. Every business would still have to pay a higher wage to get the best workers.

But, free market means free without force, meaning if someone want to work for a dollar a day with room and board why shouldn't they have that right, because when this welfare state is flat broke and can't borrow another dine it may take something like that just to survive.

Number two, "All government free aid on an individual basis must be kept separated from the free market place national economy" because that is what causes consumer inflation and unreasonable prices. And the only way to keep free unearned government handout spending on an individual basis from subsiding price raising and contaminating the free market national economy is for government to use tokens or script and operate its own commissaries, housing, and clinics.

With unearned individual government spending being kept separate and not subsiding price raising no merchant can charge more than the poor and working class can afford because of their number, there is never enough rich to support an economy.

This way the poor and working class will be able to buy the bare necessities of food and medical care, and those that falls through the crack will get tokens or script as to not freeze or starve. This economic survival plan is not perfect but it is sound and will prevent total chaos.

The welfare state has spoiled a lot of people and following this plan won't be easy and will cause much hardship and pain, but, almost anything is better than losing our freedom forever or mired in total chaos.

With the minimum wage gone people will be free to barter or do whatever it takes to survive because a broke government may be lucky just to provide national defense, internally and externally.

This country has never known anything but freedom, and I assure you without the minimum wage blocking self-help the people will barter and do whatever it take to legally save themselves and the nation.
SIRMANS LOG: 27 MAY 2012, 0042 HOURS
PS: As always I don't expect my great supernatural wisdom to be taken seriously but positive human effort is never wasted.

HE/SHE IS OUR SOB!
One thing about Nixon is in private he was known for very colorful language. In one case one of his aides was branded on and on how bad he was. I'm paraphrasing Nixon's reply: "Sure, he is a SOB, but he is
our SOB."

So, the message here to all conservatives is: The socialist/liberal news media propaganda attack machine is definitely going to brand from bottom to top anyone with any conservative leaning a SOB.

But, the fact is as long as one keep pounding until the cows come home lower taxes, more jobs, and strong national defense that will be their armor plated protection.

Then no matter what they are labeled or branded there will still be more than enough freedom loving Americans to carry the day, and say he is our SOB with their vote.
SIRMANS LOG: 22 MAY 2012, 1222 HOURS

ADD ON INJECTION: 22 MAY 2012, 2118 HOURS
It is impossible to save a country or its economy when its government prevents big business failures. That prevents any way to get rid of

waste, decay, and inefficiency. Doing that put's the whole country at risk by weighing down and crowding out positive new growth until a collapse is unavoidable.

Nature's supreme law of "Natural selection" doesn't hit any one on the head with a hammer, but nothing escapes it effect. "You can't get blood out of a turnip" for a simple reason, there is none there. It's the same with a broke government, soon its not going to take care of the elderly or anyone simply because there will be no money there.

The welfare state days are over and anyone disagreeing is simply economically ignorant and in a state of denial. Business profit is government's only means of support directly or indirectly, but by government promoting waste, decay, and inefficiency unabated soon it will be impossible for businesses to make a profit.

Knowing businesses can't make a profit

won't stop government from draining the last one dry. The reason is government sees itself as the great lord and master super social and family provider, plus the fear factor lets the politician know the masses will be coming with the pitch forks when no more government hand outs are forth coming.

Still, nothing is written in stone man still has the power to choose his destiny.

With all of these polls and figures flying around now-a-days I never forget, "Figures don't lie, but liars sure can figure."
ADD ON INJECTION END

WRITERS OPINION: LIBERALS ARE GOOD AND DECENT AMERICANS, TOO. Liberals are not bad people, almost all of my friends and relatives are liberals. In fact liberals in their minds mean well and have good intentions, but, the way to hell is paved with good intentions. Their

problem as a rule is they are just plain shallow and lack perspective.
Liberalism is a modern phenomenon.

In the distance past just the day to day struggle to survive made almost everyone conservative. Back then you had better instill accountability and responsibility in your young if you wanted any left because nature and the elements were cruel, harsh, and unforgiving.

There was no so called safety net. But, in modern time especially with our welfare state far too many people think the world owes them a living. Far too many people have what is called a weak survival instinct due to a lack of hardship and struggle.

I happen to believe that good judgment and good character goes hand in hand. Many may disagree but I believe that there must be at lease some real or imposed hardship and struggle to build good character. By saying imposed that could mean discipline or just taking away privileges.

If one has a weak survive instinct I just don't think they are equipped with the judgment to safe guard and protect future generations. No wonder they are murdering future children in the womb by the millions.

The lack of enough people with good sound strong judgment in my view is sealing our fate; after all you can't get blood out of a turnip.

Before the "New deal" and the welfare state it was mostly the rich that were morally bankrupt, very few of the poor believed in and aborted unborn children.

But, now the poorest of the poor is murdering the unborn in the womb faster than anyone, especially African American women, God bless their souls.
SIRMANS LOG: 19 MAY 2012, 2018 HOURS

A SURE CONSERVATIVE POKER WINNING HAND IN NOVEMBER 2012

I don't care if my advice is ever taken seriously; my duty is to keep pounding out my great wisdom.

Trying to out shout and do attack damage to a popular liberal is a losing strategy, mainly because maybe as much as 95 percent of the American population is economically ignorant. I believe less than five percent of the American people even know or understand where all government income originates from.

Attacking a popular liberal is sort of like attacking Santa Claus, but, more and more people are waking up to Santa Claus spending this nation into total oblivion. Still, attacking Santa Claus won't win you a popularly contest.

My advice is to forget about attacking someone else and what they have done or may not do and make sure the people know what you plan to do. That is the way Reagan did it. That is the surest way to defeat a popular liberal. Otherwise, to keep attacking and be all over the map no one will know what to expect from you.

They know at least the sugar daddy liberals are going to give away the candy store even if the nation can't afford it. The only way a conservative is going to defeat a very popular liberal in today's climate is to stop all of this attacking and keep pounding your own message of lower taxes, more jobs, and strong national defense and nothing else.

I'm not running for anything and can't make anyone take my advice. Polls and that kind of stuff is a distraction in itself that the TV pundits and talking heads gets off on.

The fact is if a conservative just stay with the said three things and nothing more until the cows come home he will win. Otherwise, the poll distortions and socialist/liberal news media propaganda attack machine will make him toast. You see what

happened to Dole and McCain, take heed.
SIRMANS LOG: 16 MAY 2012, 2029 HOURS

WILL CIVILIZATION RETURN TO THE STONE AGE?
In life with few exceptions the rule is: "No guts no glory, no risk no gain." There is a simple reason why it is impossible for an economy to work properly when government is too involved. Government acts against the laws of nature, and especially natures' supreme law of "Natural selection."

It's very simple; government stops and prevents the elimination of waste, decay, and inefficiency. You can't have life, growth, or lasting progress being bogged down with waste, decay, and inefficiency. You
see, government doesn't adhere to

supply and demand; it operates only on force and power.

Whereas, a free market place economy with unrestrictive competition will supply far more than any nation can use or demand. Believe it or not, the main reason why is it does something a pure communist or socialist system will never do.

Free competition is the stick to get rid of inefficiency, and allowing an unlimited individual reward motivates the most power energy packed force in our entire human makeup, that energy force is greed.

People without wisdom and perspective will never understand this but there is no other force in our human makeup with enough motivation to produce more jobs, food, and everything else than any one nation can use.

Sure, like electricity greed is very dangerous, but free competition bridles it without forceful eliminating or shutting it down completely like communism and socialism does. We use to have this great freedom in the USA, but with the "New deal" and our welfare state we are well on our way to being a communist or socialist state.

It is simple; there has never been and never will be a rich and wealthy country with job for almost everyone without a lot of greedy rich and wealthy entrepreneurs to make it happen. Rich people are not the same as poor people with money, there is a world of difference in attitude.

People naturally have different talents and abilities and should always have the same opportunity, but to always receive the same result in life (reward) is stupid and against the laws of nature. But, generally that is what a communist and socialist state promotes.

That is why government should never be heavily involved in the operations of private businesses. Government is always going to reward its friend and punish its perceived enemies. In a democracy governments job is to collect only enough taxes to protect the nation and the upkeep of the infrastructure, period.

It is not government's duty to be a social and family provider from cradle to grave. In my view government as a social and family provider is like eating your seed corn or even more horrible eating your young.

Before the "New deal" government acting as a nanny state had never been done on a mass scale in the history of mankind. It destroys a nation's culture, nuclear and extended family system, and any emergency capacity to barter.

That is a total destruction of the foundation for human survival; western civilization has little left of those 5,000 year pillars of support. When we fall no one knows where it will end, the Stone Age is not an impossibility.

Still, with my great wisdom and insight
I'm seen as a nut case, fool, and
a throwback to the eighteenth century
that don't know what the hell
I'm talking about. The only thing I can
say about that is: I pray to God
you are right and I'm wrong. God bless
the USA.
SIRMANS LOG: 15 MAY 2012, 1051 HOURS

JUST LIBERAL PROPAGANDA BACKGROUND NOISE!
There has never been and never will be
a pure communist or socialist
state that could feed its entire people
home grown without natural
resources to sell. So, to all of these
economic ignorant people that hate
capitalism, rich people, and big
business, be careful of what you wish
for because unless drastic changes are
made you are going to get it.

Unless my deep wisdom advice is
taken which the egg heads will never

do means your wish will be granted sooner than you think. The reason is freedom and democracy demands responsibility, accountability, and people with sound judgment, which fewer and fewer has in this great nation today.

Soon when the boom is finally lowered there will only be two choices left, total chaos or total authority, history has shown there will be no compromised middle ground.

Damn, nobody is listening, my God; this dumb idea that one has to refute every single little charge against you in a political race is just plain nonsense. I don't think, in fact I know you can't make hateful negative people like you no matter what you do.

I am a firm believer that if one dwell on doing what he feel is fair and right people of decency and goodwill will accept you for who you are and what you stand for. But, to deny and be overly concerned about every little negative charge by liberals

that only want to destroy you is
an exercise in futility.

People don't love you because you are
perfect people love you because
you are human caring and decent.
People got eyes, they can see
unfairness from the liberal propaganda
attack machine, and they will
ignore it if the intended victim will
ignore it.

It will be just like water off a ducks
back if one ignores it and keep
pounding low taxes, more jobs, and
strong national defense. Otherwise,
if the intended victim can't ignore it
then the people can't ignore it
either and will detect weakness, which
is not good.

Just make only one statement to any
new charge and get back to pounding
and pounding your message.

Like Nixon said, "The haters can't
destroy you unless you hate them
back, then you destroy yourself." This
lean and mean liberal news media

propaganda attack machine takes no conservative political prisoners.

That is just the way it is in this knockout drag out battle for this nations survival as a free nation. This is it folks, this is for all the marbles, there will be no tomorrow for individual freedom in this great nation.

I'm in the fray folks, I don't want to be, but this is my beloved home the only home I know. So be it, destiny is calling on my great wisdom and perspective.
SIRMANS LOG: 10 MAY 2012, 2359 HOURS

A WELFARE STATE IS LIKE AN INCESTUOUS RELATIONSHIP! Economically wise a welfare state may be compared to an incestuous relationship. In a normal free market place economy private enterprise generate the profit with little to no government interference.

Through taxing the government takes

off the top only a small cut needed to protect the nation and maintain the infrastructure. That way the economic process and everything else functions normally.

Nature's supreme law of "Natural selection" keeps all prices under control by maintaining a balance between the merchant and the consumer. But, in life there is always going to be people that fall through the cracks like the poor and disadvantage.

Throughout history until the "New deal" came along the nuclear and extended family system, the church, and community organizations aided these people. It was not a perfect system but it was the best system known to man for well over six thousand years.

Just like life itself it had a rebirth and death cycle known as booms and busts. Then, here comes liberal do-gooder geniuses that think they can take all of the risk out of life. Life can't exist without risk because there must be someway to get rid of waste, decay, and inefficiency. They didn't realize that nature's supreme law of "Natural selection" is based on a survival need for anything to exist over time.

Now, we as a nation are putting all of our faith in and depending on one super sugar daddy provider government from cradle to grave to survive. Thereby taking away a survival need for a system that has been around well over six thousand years, how dumb can we get?

More and more there is no survival need for the once strong nuclear and extended family, or to have good morals and values, that is why they are slowly ceasing out of existence. There is no wonder why men are marring men and women are marring women.

I could go on and on for hours on the damage the welfare state has done to our economy, our morals, our

values, and everything else we use to hold dear. But I will end by saying: I believe we as a nation are sc...... ourselves incestuously. Great solution to the problem is found throughout my writing and books, Freddie L. Sirmans, Sr.
SIRMANS LOG: 09 MAY 2012, 1208 HOURS

GOVERNMENT INDIVIDUAL SPENDING MUST BE KEPT SEPARATE FROM THE NATION'S ECONOMY IF IT IS TO BE SAVED.
The reason I pound so hard for government to separate all of its individual spending and get the hell completely out of the nation's free market place is because that is the main thing killing our economy.

The stock market and all of that other stuff is just side issues.
Government involvement is what's killing the economy that is why I stress so hard that government must start using tokens or script when aiding the poor and disadvantage on

an individual basis.

That will prevent government spending from contaminating the national economy. Sure, we must not let people freeze and starve but the only way government can aid the poor and disadvantage without destroying the free market place economy is by operating its own commissaries, housing, and clinics system with the use of tokens or script to keep that spending separate.

The destructive system we are using now takes tax money from one group of Americans, and then in competition against we the tax payers gives that money to another less producing group which results in higher and higher prices and taxes on everyone.

That is why tokens or script must be used for all government spending that is done on an individual basis, that would keep merchants from raising prices higher and higher on everyone, which is the reason for the consumer inflation we have today.

The main way this contamination occurs is when government gives out masses amounts of money on an individual basis. That infusion of mass amount of unearned (government spending is unearned spending) money allows merchant to raising prices higher and higher against ourselves we the tax payers.

The government subsides price raising on everyone by giving out masses amount of money and food stamps to the poor and disadvantage on an individual basis, there is not enough rich and others to support too high prices.

Without that government subsidy to the poor and disadvantage, basic food and medical prices could never go higher than the poor could afford.

So, instead of subsiding higher prices on everyone in helping the poor, the poor and disadvantage can still be helped without the government driving up prices, if only government would use tokens or script in its own government operated support systems.

Making the government use tokens of script for all individual government spending would stop this nonsense, as you see, economic ignorance is staring us in the face.

So, in closing this chapter, I repeat, for this nation and our economy to survive all government spending done on an individual basis tokens or script must be used, period. God! I ask in you name, save our great nation.
SIRMANS LOG: 08 MAY 2012, 0958 HOURS

CAUTION! CONSERVATIVES THINK BEFORE YOU LEAP!
Warning! Stop! Don't! For now don't cut or reduce spending or anything else. It will only reduce the size of the pie and make everything worse and maybe even instantly wreck the

economy.

A smaller pie means fewer jobs and everything else, and it may even double the dole population and push the debt from 16 trillion to 32 trillion. Government spending ain't the problem it is how it is doing the spending.

It shouldn't but if government is going to do social and provider spending anyway it should be done by providing government commissaries, government housing, and government clinic with the use of tokens or script.

Government get the hell out of private enterprise and let private enterprise and the free market place sink or swim on its own, this is an order. To kick start and get this whole process rolling right now eliminate the minimum wage.

The welfare state era is over. Government in the role of social and family provider has out lived its time. Profit from American businesses is the only thing that supports our government either from directly taxing business or indirectly from the wages paid to business employees and their property.

Let's describe business profit as your seed corn. When government is small and taking care of only national defense and infrastructure like parks, roads, and bridges it only needs to take a small amount of business seed corn profit. That way the business will have plenty left to raise and grow another bumper crop.

But, when government takes on a social and family provider role it rapidly grows government demanding it take bigger and bigger chunks of businesses seed corn profit. The bigger chunk government takes the less seed corn the business will have to grow another crop.

Our government welfare state as social and family provider now has grown so large there is not enough business seed corn profit available for the welfare state to take to survive without killing off American business. That is what this liberal created social and family provider government has brought this great nation too.

There is no foreign invader, we are now face to face with the enemy, and it is economic ignorance. We are now at economic death door, we no longer have a choice, we either separate all government spending from our free enterprise economic system or the economy will definitely collapse and freedom in this nation will be lost forever.

This can be done by the government not giving anyone money unless they work for the government, also no food stamps. Of course the government must help people and not let people freeze or starve.

But, government must do that by operating government run commissaries, housing, and clinics with the use of tokens or script, but there must be a separation, otherwise it will be impossible for our less than free market place economy to survive.

Also, we must as a nation eliminates the minimum wage, that way the people can save themselves. A half a loaf is better than nothing because all of the supposedly safety nets won't have the funds to save anyone.
It coming folks, this government is broke and the sooner that sinks in the better.

Right now to the masses of government dependents that kind of talk about economic failure is just pesky noise. Lord save this great nation. Folks, I know my drum beat to eliminate the minimum wage don't seem to make sense, but I have the wisdom and perspective to know it is the only way out.

A minimum wage is a forced manipulation of the free market which means we don't have a free market place economy. If we did we wouldn't be in the sad shape we are in. Without a forced minimum wage the whole economy would be in balance.

With no minimum wage labor and cost would balance each other allowing the very poor to afford and pay their own food and medical bills, which now is impossible. The minimum wage ain't free, people don't realize it but it just forces a business to charge more for everything you buy.

Sure, in moderation a higher wage is not a bad thing, but when has a government handout ever stopped with moderation. Besides, it is done by force and that is totally against the rules of a free market place economy.
SIRMANS LOG: 7 MAY 2012, 1527 HOURS

CURRENT EVENT INJECTION: 3 MAY 2012, 2333 HOURS
Whoa! Maybe I'm crazy and it's just me! Or maybe I'm just missing something here! Or maybe it's just a

liberal thing! When did we as a nation become proud to air our dirty linen in public! Sure, sometimes you gotta do what you gotta do, but, who says you have to publically wallow in it? What happened, it has always been the American way to use a big stick and walk silently. CURRENT EVENT INJECTION END: SIRMANS LOG: 3 MAY 2012, 2345 HOURS

UPDATED: 2 MAY 2012, 1827 HOURS
THE MIGHTY LIBERAL PROPAGANDA ATTACK MACHINE IN ACTION IS AN AWESOME POWER!
The big horse race coming up in November in my view will determine the survival of western civilization. To take the golden crown for the conservatives it is going to take a no holds barred knock down drag out political battle like no one has ever seen in this country.

Get the women, children, and old folks off the streets, which, I'm sure, disqualifies me and my views up front.

Standing between whoever takes the crown is a dug in hardcore battle harden predominate liberal news media that sees self-sufficiency and old fashion traditional family values as the enemy.

The all powerful liberal news media has brain washed ninety five percent of the American people to some degree to believe the welfare state will always be around to take care of everybody instead of every man feeling responsible for his own survival.

The might of the liberal propaganda machine aimed at any conservative is an awesome sight of raw power. When it hits a conservative even some hardcore conservatives may ease up and not speak as freely their true convictions, let alone pretenders who may end up trying to out liberal a liberal.

No matter how many so called power brokers bet on the horse they think can take the crown it ain't gonna happen unless that horse hold to conservative values. The biggest weakness of the all powerful liberal news media propaganda attack machine is their conviction that they are right and that most Americans agree with them.

They are dead wrong on that, as a rule whatever the liberal news media believes the American people believe just the opposite. But, people are human and when they are bombarded and pounded over and over with the same liberal propaganda it has an effect. And it will carry the day, especially it you don't have a genuine conservative with the guts to push back tit for tat.

With the liberal attack machine constant on guard ready to pounce, the smartest thing any conservative can do is select only about three things to dwell on and nothing more.

Sure, it will get boring and people will be saying I know that and I am tired of hearing that and they may tune out but they won't forget the three things you stand for, otherwise being all over the map the liberal propaganda attack machine will make sure no one knows what the hell you stand for.

Grab a sound bite for lower taxes, better job opportunities, and keeping a strong national defense. Just like a pit bull bite down on those three things and never ease up come hell or high waters.

If a conservative keep it simple and refuse to get dispersed all over the map he will take the crown. But, if he starts watching all of the polls and listening to all of the liberal defeatist propaganda he may start thinking and acting like a loser, which can then become a reality.

I've seen in action the awesome power of the liberal propaganda attack machine in taking out Dole and then McCain, and believe me the stage is set for a repeat. Even now no one can really tell you what either of those candidates truly stood for, pro or con, simply because they were all over the map.

The only way to get through this mine field is to keep it simple, bore the hell out of the people with not more than three proven conservative winners. Like the old football technique, "Three and a half yards and a cloud of dust," everybody in the stands knew what you were going to do but the opposition couldn't stop you.

The same applies here, Pound and pound sound bites on low taxes, more jobs, and strong nation defense and nothing else until the cows come home. Otherwise, the liberal propaganda attack machine will disperse your message and label you to their liking and smash you like a bug.

It is a mine game; too, the attack machine armed with polls, the special interest, and others will be hollering and whooping it up to pry you loose from those three proven winners.

Like any winning coach will tell you, you can never guarantee you will win, the most you can do in any game is be in a position to win, then the odds are in your favor because on a given day luck is as much a part of the game as anything else.

And For-God-Sake forget about details, all that does is give the liberal propaganda attack machine fodder and ammo for propaganda to confirm the cold heartless uncaring label they are trying to make stick.

Just layout the three things you are going to do and keep pounding them until the cows come home. How you are going to do this and how are you going to do that will only be taken out of context and distorted to drown out your real massages.

Forget about reasoning, you can't reason with liberals, they don't care about logic and reason; their only care is to win in anyway and at any cost. A genuine responsible person would self-sacrifice and put country above all personal interest, but with the shape this country is in all the blame can't be placed just on liberals.

In fact ninety five percent of the general population in the country is still asleep with unshakable faith in uncle sugar and has no idea of the dire shape this country is in, our freedom and way of life is at deaths door and less then five percent of the population even realize it. Lord, have mercy on our souls.

Sure, the Madison Avenue boys and girls along with the party pollster's and experts will be totally against what I am saying, but, I stand by my analysis.

Trying to out shout and stay one upper on a liberal tends not to work because subconsciously people know that generally liberals lack a very deep sense of responsibility. And they tend not to hold liberals to as high a standard as a conservative.

The independents will never desert one
that will stick only to low taxes,
more jobs, and strong national defense
if they know he is sincere. But,
to be lured off into chasing after
women issues, gay issues, who killed
who, and every other Tom, Dick, and
Harry liberal outcry imaginable is
just what the liberal attack machine
wants.

The sensible thing to do with a new
outcry is make only one policy
statement, and stand by it by telling
the distractors my first statement
stands. Then get back to pounding and
pounding low taxes, more jobs,
and a strong national defense.
Otherwise, the liberal propaganda
attack machine will keep you away
from your bread and butter message
forever

Whoa here! I hear more liberal
claptrap, this anti wealth mentality that
is in the liberal mind is just that,
because it just doesn't pan out in
practice. There is something in the

makeup of the human psyche that attracts people to bigger than life stuff.

For some unknown reason pomp, ceremony, extravaganza, and all of that kind of crazy nonessential stuff have an attraction and pulling effect on people. I really don't know why, but I suspect that it has something to do with the allure of power. There is just something that attracts people to that kind of stuff.

Look at all of the worshiping of movie stars and big time sport figures. Evangelism is big business in this country today with mega-churches, but one of the lessons learned by the early evangelist was how to build a big following.

They learned that one could be the best preacher with the best message and that alone may get you some followers, but it took more to build a Hugh following. And one effective way was to be seen as bigger than life with pomp, expensive flashy cars, fine pews, fine churches &

furniture, and fine flashy clothes.

I think most seniors have heard of Daddy Grace and other early evangelist. So, all I'm saying is living high on the hog doesn't necessarily turn most people off. Who it actually turns off is those with a something for nothing socialist mentality.

The reason I wrote this article is because the socialist/liberal news media propaganda attack machine was trying to stir up resentment among the people, because someone with their own hard earned money was proud of the cars they could afford.

Poor hard working Americans has never resented rich people enjoying the good life. In fact they want that, too. In America anything is still possible, that is if we can keep these socialist from taking over.

Just remember the story about the Woodchopper; he was trying to split an extra tough might oak block. He hit the blade of his big axe time and time again on this particular block. After a while he felt there was no use and decided to give up.

But, at the last minute before walking away he decided to kneel down and take a closer look. And to his surprise he could see a small split. The moral of the story is: Positive human effort is never wasted. Many times we may feel it doesn't really matter and we are just wasting our time on something.

So many times over the years with my writing I have felt it is a curse, I haven't made any money at it, and felt nobody really cares and it all a waste of time. But, the thing with me is I don't know how to be a quitter and I'm still at it.

All of my life I have been written off dismissed and seen as someone destiny to be a failure in life, but, by the grace of God here I am still standing at age seventy, three days before this Christmas 2012.

As you can see, I am in favor of restoring old fashion values to this nation, I may not be right, but this is my analysis on what it will take to grab the golden crown and save western civilization.
SIRMANS LOG: 21 APRIL 2012, 1806 HOURS

READ MY SHORT RAW NO CHASER LECTURE ON SIRMANS ECONOMICS! It never ceases to amaze me on just how economically ignorant most people are. This whole modern generation is looking to big government to always be there to take care of them. But, the true fact is the government is only a necessary parasite that every organized society must have to defend and protect its citizens.

An Economy consists of only to parties, a seller and a buyer or a merchant and a consumer. Nature's supreme law of "Natural selection" balances these two forces against each other where prices can never get out of hand.

If government just take a small amount off the top a balance can still be maintained, but, when government takes too much of the cream of profit the incentive to produce heads downward. The government doesn't generate any profit and every penny it takes in taxes to survive originates from some form of private business transaction.

It is either directly or indirectly. Non business people that pay taxes to the government all receive their pay from some form of private business transaction profit. So, what have we now, a general public that see government as some kind of imaginary omnipotent sow with countless tits that we can suck on forever.

Besides, a business doesn't pay taxes anyway; a business is just a medium of exchange and nothing else. It is a medium of exchange between a buyer and a seller with the seller being the owner of the product or service. The exchange between the seller (owner) and the buyer must produce a profit for the owner otherwise all of the owner's labor would be for nothing.

So, when the government comes in and taxes the owner's profit that tax must be passed on to the buyer (customer) in the form of higher prices. You see, when the government taxes a business it is simply indirectly taxing the public or a part of it in the form of higher prices, that is what is called consumer inflation.

When the tax is small there is not much of a problem, but when the bite becomes too great especially along with mountains of government red tape, unemployment and mass business failure is the result.

That is sheer madness and to top that we have this liberal anti-business climate that bites the hand that feeds it. My God! It is a case of the parasite attacking the host that keeps it alive, how dumb and stupid can it get? This is what the shallow minded liberals and their welfare state has done to this great predominate Christian nation.

There has never been a mass social and family provider government in the history of mankind before the "New deal" came along. The profits from private enterprise are what supports government and can keep government supplied as long as government limits its spending to national defense and the infrastructure.

But, the profit from private business can never be enough to support a social and provider government very long. The welfare state days are over, it is no mystery to me, there is simply not enough business profit to pay the cost, and you can't get blood out of a turnip, period. And anybody that think that we as a nation can continue with our welfare state is living in fantasy land, period.

It is simply impossible to pay the cost, we are broke people, and still we have politicians in washing acting like we are a rich nation. We are over 16 trillion in debt and still trying to spend like drunken sailors.

The egg heads with their scrambled brains and the elite will never change course they are in a state of denial and will go down with the ship first. Why they call them eggheads in the first place is because their brains are scrambled, with common sense nowhere to be found. And I'm supposed to be the fool and nut case and maybe I am, but at least I have enough common sense to know we are headed toward total doom.

I write what I think and believe, so I hope my short lecture will enlighten at least one soul somewhere out there and everyone won't think I am totally insane.

When I talk about economics I'm

talking about a free market place. There has never been a communist or socialist form of government that could feed all of it people. In those types of governments the top leadership lives high on the hog while the general population barley keeps from starving.
SIRMANS LOG: 30 MARCH 2012, 0017 HOURS

QUICK WORD OF KNOWLEDGE INJECTION:
Economically speaking caring for the poor or anybody must be kept separated for a free market place to work, that is the problem now, you can't have unlimited individual government spending standing between the merchants and the consumers and expect a healthy sound free market place economy. What you will have is uncontrolled consumer inflation like what is taking place now, that and the "Minimum wage" is the fuel that is spinning consumer inflation out of control.

There is no way in the hell to stop this economy from expanding beyond control and collapse from it own weight with the course it is on. You don't have to take my advice; the wait won't be very much longer. Government must sell off damn near everything and give up its social and family provider role, period. Will it happen, no?

If the USA government doesn't eliminate the "Minimum wage and give up its social and family provider role will the USA economy survive, no. So, what is going to happen to this great land of the free and home of the brave, you really don't want to know the answer to that as I see it.

Well, if you insist and won't take no for an answer I guess I have no choice but to tell you what I think is going to happen. I believe to buy time and avoid biting the dust our Welfare State and the Federal Reserve as co-conspirators will finish selling off what is left of our freedom and sovereignty to some foreign highest bidder like a cheap street walker. And we will end up as debt slaves.

So, how you like me now?
SIRMANS LOG: Last update 27 MARCH 2012, 1613 HOURS

DOES IT REALLY MATTER WHO WINS IN NOVEMBER???
NEW INJECTION 1
I know people are thinking what about the government paying off this
or that and who is going to lose this or that. This nation is way past that
now we are now in a priority struggle on whether this nation and
freedom will survive or be lost forever.

To continue on the doomsday course we are on now soon nothing is
going to get paid anyway because we may not even have a country. The
shallow minded liberals starting with the "New deal" got this nation in
the fix we are in, and even to this day won't accept responsibility for
anything but instead can blame the

sweetness out ginger bread.

Hell, the liberal ain't over twenty percent of the population, but they are super aggressive, if you get between a liberal and a cause you are going to get trampled if you ain't got your s... together. These people will stop at nothing, morally or otherwise to stay in power.

Someway somehow conservatives must snatch the reins from these people otherwise we are all going over the cliff or down the tube. God save our freedom.
20 MARCH 2012, 2226 HOURS

If you want my opinion, which no one has asked, but, guess what, I'm going to give it anyway. We have a milestone election coming up in November and I believe it will determine whether we as a nation lose our freedom quickly or go the drip by drip route.

The drip by drip course is the best

course only because it buys more time for a miracle to possibly save our freedom. OK, OK, what if we do get a new team? What will it do about the welfare state entitlement load?

Will it have the guts to actually lighten the welfare state massive financial load? Sure, I have heard promises about cutting government spending but it ain't gonna happen, the welfare state is simply just too powerful. Besides, in my view making massive cuts in government spending would do more harm than good because all it would do is increase the dole roll?

The problem is government as a social and family provider simply doesn't work and it is impossible to keep it from collapsing soon. The only thing that is going to save the USA and western civilization is to somehow get the government out of its social and family provider role, period.

Otherwise, I don't care what those in

powers tell you the USA economy
can't be saved, I know almost no one
will believe me, and why should
they, an unknown writer like me can't
possibly know jack. An economy
is like life itself there must be constant
small purges and rebirths taking
place for it to stay healthy.

The free market place ideology allows
that to take place better than any
other economic system known to man.
Governments tend not to adhere
to supply and demand and will use its
power to stop small purges and
will reward its friends, thereby choking
off healthy small purges and
rebirth.

This process won't kill an economy on
the spot but will cause it to
wither and die on the vine, which is
what is happening to the USA and
welfare states all over the world.
Growth itself is a process of birth and
death; otherwise there would be no
lasting life.

The welfare state is what is going to

destroy the USA and western civilization unless they get out of their social and provider roles. The nuclear and extended family unit is what civilization is based on. It is the foundation of all civilization.

Before the "New deal" the head of household was not only a provider he instilled in the young self-restraint, responsibility, and accountability. The "New deal" birthed the welfare state we have today.

The welfare state on a massive scale has taken the family provider role away from where it had been for over 5,000 years, with each nuclear family unit head of household.

That in itself wasn't so bad but what was so destructive even to this day is government as family provider is not making sure the young is instilled with self-restraint, responsibility, and accountability. Only the provider has the power and authority to make sure the young are prepared to be productive future adults.

Today with the poor it is not uncommon to see grand and great grand mothers having to raise young kids. I just highlighted a sample of the destruction the welfare state has done just on our culture. Moving on to some of the destruction the welfare state has done to our economy.

The founding fathers knew what an all powerful big government would do they had seen it back in old Europe. They knew that the only way to control government was to keep it small. The constitution is all about limiting the power of government over the people.

The constitution gave the greatest power to the people and to the states. The state governors use to have awesome powers. Each state governor appointed two senators to represent his and the state's interest.

Then because of petty politics, with the 17th amendment the states gave up their real power by not having two appointed senators to represent only state business and interest, now special interest may have more influence with the senators than the state governor. And the people gave up their real power by allowing the government to take over the family provider role for itself.

Now the all powerful welfare state with little to no real opposition is busy consolidating its massive power to finish selling off the little sovereign power the USA has left. Within five years the USA will be an economic slave in my opinion, now chew on that.

Whoever is the provider has the power to be the boss, yes sir. In economic terms the only thing that truly matters is profit. You can be spinning your wheels and kicking up all kinds of dust but if you are not making any profit you ain't going anywhere.

As a country when we are borrowing

forty cents of every dollar we spend we are definitely profit challenged. Every cent the government takes comes from some type of private business transaction. When government is small it only needs to take a small amount out of a businesses profit margin. But, the bigger government grows the more it must take from the profit a business makes.

This welfare state we have won't stop until its bite is so big no business can make a profit, there is no stopping the greed of a welfare state. It don't make any sense, that doesn't matter, most of the stuff taking place now don't make any sense in my view.

No matter who wins the election if they are not willing to get the government out of its super provider role it will not save this economy. Here is what should be done, first eliminate the "Minimum wage."

Next set up government run

commissaries, government housing, and government run clinics with the use of token or script for those that qualify.

Lastly, government must stop giving out free money or food stamps to anyone, that is what driver consumer inflation and keeps prices sky high for everyone.
SIRMANS LOG: 18 MARCH 2012, 0014 HOURS

STOP MASS MURDER OF THE INNOCENT IN THE WOMB
What few people understand about freedom and a free market place is it works both ways; there must be freedom to succeed or fail, and freedom to pay the most in wages or the least.

That is what freedom means, without force in any direction that is what nature's supreme law of "Natural selection" is all about, without force, let nature's law of "Natural selection" decide. That means an employer should have the right to pay as much or as little as he wants to as long as no force is involved, no one has to accept it.

The greatest and mightiest of giant oak trees started as a small acorn.
The ability to start small is what real growth is all about. Before all of the big government welfare states bars and hoops one has to jump through now any poor person with initiative could pull himself up by his own boot straps.

Now starting from almost nothing is becoming almost impossible and is only going to get worse. Sure, I write a lot of extreme stuff, which to a large extent is to stress a point, but, I know the secret to life is all about balance and common sense.

Like in time of old, the people knew without a doubt that certain things doesn't chance with time and one of those things was building character.

We as humans have evolved over millions of years through hardship and struggle. And I just don't believe that a strong survival instinct along with good judgment and character can be instilled in the young without a certain amount of real or imposed hardship and struggle.

Of all the crimes against nature the welfare state has done I think the biggest of all is its corruption of the poor. Never in the history of mankind has the poor been moral corrupted on such a mass scale and is out there killing babies in the womb by the millions, may God bless their souls.
SIRMANS LOG: 15 MARCH 2012, 1425 HOURS

LET THE SUPREME COURT RULE ON THE CONSTITUTIONALITY OF THE "MINIMUM WAGE."
Mandates, mandates, individual mandates, and mandates to no end. When it comes to individual mandates to make everyone buy health

insurance or go to jail I am against that along with almost everyone.

Well, what about one of the first individual government mandates, I'm talking about the "Minimum wage, that was one of the welfare states first mandates. Without the minimum wage the welfare state could never have taken over and grown into this all powerful monster we have today that is going to spend this nation into oblivion.

If I am willing to work for someone just for room and board why shouldn't I have that right? If I am willing to pay all of someone's expense and pay them a dollar a day why shouldn't they have a right to say yes/no.

In today's climate I know it would be a miracle to pass a Supreme Court decision, still, I think it should be put to a Supreme Court test. As you can see, I am totally against a "Minimum wage" I think getting rid of the minimum wage especially at this

late stage is the only thing that will save the USA and western civilization, period.
SIRMANS LOG: 14 MARCH 2012, 2041 HOURS

WHAT IS MORAL DECAY? DUH!
One of the reasons I am so misunderstood is because I have a super strong survival instinct, whereas today due to the welfare state most Americans has a dependency weak survival instinct.

You first have to know and be able to recognize a moral threat before you can truly take someone like me serious, I am mostly dismissed and seen as some kind of nut case talking a lot of hate filled nonsense.
Which, couldn't be farther from the truth.

I understand this because not all has paid the price in struggle and suffering that I have to instill a super survival instinct. But, history is my guide and without a doubt will prove me right.

Anything that doesn't protect the unborn and future generations is a moral threat in my eyes, by instinct alone I just know, no one has to tell me. A moral threat doesn't physical kill you on the spot but over time it is just as dangerous, your species will cease to exist.

No sovereign country can continue to depend forty percent on another and stay free and independent for very long. Almost everyone is totally focused on the lack of jobs and the economy while what is coming in low under the radar is just as destructive.

I am talking about moral decay and culture rot. Anyone with any knowledge of history should know that moral decay and culture rot is the last stage before a nation will be taken over or conquered.

Throughout history the only real security for women, children, the elderly, and everyone else has been with a strong nuclear and extended family system. But, here we are as a nation putting all of our faith in a welfare state that is on life support, God help us.

Almost the whole nation is in mass denial from being brainwashed for decades by a liberal bias news media in my view. I am totally in favor of women rights as well as rights for all Americans, but there is not going to be rights for any of us if we don't first save our nuclear and extended family system and our culture.

This country's government is borrowing forty cents out of every dollar it spends, and what is even worse is nothing is being done about it, and even super worse is we have a liberal bias media that is on the sideline cheering the process on, God save us.

No country with a culture like we had before the "New deal" would tolerate this behavior for one second, which is proof of what this welfare state beast has done to our once great culture.

The moral decay and culture rot due to our welfare state has just grown too powerful; only the elimination of the "Minimum wage" will set in motion a process that will save the United States of America.
SIRMANS LOG: 11 MARCH 2012, 1425 HOURS

CURRENT EVENT INJECTION:
THERE IS BLOOD IN THE WATER AND THE LIBERAL SHARKS ARE CIRCLING! The great conservative radio talk show host has admitted that he slipped up and has apologized for the infractions. He is not the first one to get caught up in emotion and stray over the line and will not be the last.

However, the progressive liberals smell blood in the water and in their view see this as their opportunity to take down the biggest conservative voice of all. Sure, they already got the heat turned up enough to drive a few from the kitchen, but, in my view they are kicking around a powder keg, here.

This could rejuvenate and give life to a dying moral decaying giant that is all but dead in America. Sure, in my view the radio talk show host was wrong for his slut and prostitute name calling, but, he was right on his assault on the outrageous moral decay that is rotting to the core our once great culture.

The shallow minded liberals don't know what the hell I'm talking about concerning moral decay, they couldn't recognize a moral threat if it slapped them upside the head. I could go on and on but enough said, I say let bygones be bygones. I rest my case.
SIRMANS LOG: 6 MARCH 2012, 0024 HOURS

PS: JUST A PASSING THOUGHT, 8 march 2012, 2345 HOURS:
I think one of the major TV networks has morphed into just a plain negative anti-survival moral decay propaganda machine. I believe this

TV network has contempt and a secret hate for the strong traditional nuclear family. And especially one with a no nonsense strong male disciplinarian as head of household.

GOVERNMENT SPENDING AIN'T THE PROBLEM, HOW IT DOES THE SPENDING IS THE PROBLEM.
Just like the big powerful enemy armored divisions of WWII ran on ball bearings the welfare state runs on the "Minimum wage. So, the only way the people is ever going to regain control and save the last bastion of true freedom of the individual left in the world today is by completely eliminating the minimum wage, period.

The all powerful welfare state beast will never in its view yield one inch of its God given power back to the people; it will see this country in ashes first. It all starts with the minimum wage; I'm talking about the growth and taking over of the country by the welfare state. The minimum wage is the life blood and backbone of the welfare state.

Without the minimum there would be no out of control welfare state beast like we have today. Without the minimum wage anyone could hire the poor, the young, the handicapped, the prisoners, and many, many others without facing mountains of red tape. As it is now everyone must pay a minimum wage, and meet every other kind of government restriction one can imagine.

Without the minimum wage you wouldn't have the elderly, single women, single men, and probably a fifth of the USA population living alone. Once government got a taste of the God like power of being a super social and family provider and playing daddy without carrying out family discipline the die was cast for the destruction of our culture.

Nowhere in over five thousand years of written history has government ever been a mass social and family provider until the "New deal" came along. The government now takes from self-sacrificing hardworking producers and in many cases gives that hard earned money to lack of initiative deadbeat non-producers. My God! People are not stupid! How long will it be before the country is reduced to the lowest denominator?

Truly we are living on borrowed time. The minimum wage must go if western civilization is to survive; there are no ifs, and's, and but's about it. It is not possible for prices to rise above what the poor can afford to pay unless government is subsidizing price raising on an individual basis in some way.

Government giving anyone free money or food stamps is subsiding price raising on the general public no matter how you spin it, the result is still the same, consumer inflation. As a last resort, if the government must aid the poor it can be done without causing out of control inflation like we have today.

If government must aid the poor and disadvantage it should be done by establishing government run Commissaries, housing, and clinics and issue tokens or script to those that qualify. That will prevent out of control consumer inflation like we have today.

That will allow the rest of the working poor and others to pay for their own food and doctor bills. Then almost all of the money government takes in taxes can go to repairing bridges, the highways, city pipe and sewage systems and above all adequate national defense.

The people are suppose to be taking care of the government not the government taking care of the people, and especially not in masses like this welfare state is doing. I say to hell with the eggheads and the elites with their doomsday go down with the ship insanity, I say lets stop this suicide train to hell by first eliminating the minimum wage.

That will quickly bleed the pressure off the stuck inflationary throttle.
Then with the minimum wage no reverse restriction bar lifted a true free market place economy will kick in and back this run-a-way mother away from the cliff. Whew! Just in time! Thank God!

There is never a case in history where a real true free market place economy failed. Sure, it rebirths and renews itself but that is normal to get rid of waste and inefficiency. That is what is wrong with our welfare state, the moral decay and liberal media bias has a deadly choke hold on this nation that only a free market place with normal rebirths can break. Otherwise, a total economic collapse is imminent.

I don't need or want any credit for anything, I'm just hell bent on doing what I can to help save my homeland, the only home I know. Praise be to God.
SIRMANS LOG: 25 FEBRUARY 2012, 2140 HOURS

THE BIG LIE STIMULUS FALSE ASSUMPTION!
NEW INJECTION 2:

The reason I know without a doubt that I am right on most of the things I write about is because the economy is just like life itself; it must have a death and rebirth cycle. It is like having a normal healthy memory, in order to have that we must be able to prioritize and forget ninety nine percent of the junk and meaningless stuff we experience.

We know that oxidation work to get rid of things physically. I'm not for sure what get rid of things mentally but I do know by nature's design everything must fail or die or be renewed in some way or cease to exist.

Moral decay, inefficiency, and waste must be gotten rid of or they will become too powerful and bring down civilization itself, which could mean back to the Stone Age. The only way to save the USA is by eliminating the "Minimum wage" and reverting back to a true free market place economy with unrestricted competition.

The moral decay, the partisan liberal news media, and other anti-survival forces have become just too powerful for the USA to survive as a free people, period. Nothing except a true free market place can do the weeding without throwing out the baby with the bath water.
19 FEBRUARY 2012, 1625 HOURS

NEW INJECTION 1:
There is probably a divine reason why I keep up the drum beat of a complete elimination of the "Minimum wage." You see, man using reasoning and intelligence will never get the USA out of the economically mess the progressive liberals has gotten this nation into.

Only God and natures supreme law of "Natural selection" can save the USA and the world from total destruction back to the Stone Age. That is the reason I keep screaming, get rid of the "Minimum wage" at all cost, because I know man with his facts and figures alone will never save our civilization, it is too far gone.

There are simply just too many variables many which are subjective like whose back is being scratched, who is hiding under the desk, and on and on. That is why power hates a free market place because it prevents the handing out of goodies to cronies.

The invisible hand which is nature's supreme law of "Natural selection" in action is what ultimately rules the economy and all existence anyway. "You can't get blood out of a turnip," the laws of nature are just that simple and to think and do otherwise is a state of denial.

All the elimination of the "Minimum wage" does is set in motion what is going to ultimately happen by the force of nature anyway. But, if
Mother Nature is force to carry out its

law it could mean back to the
Stone Age.
18 FEBRUARY 2012, 0945 HOURS

I got so sick and tired of hearing this big lie about how worse off the economy would be if not for the stimulus that I just couldn't take it anymore, I just had to vent.

People getting on TV talking about how bad the economy would be
today if not for the trillions of dollars spent on the stimulus package. Nonsense, the truth is most of that spending went to phony liberal
crony capitalism anyway in my view.

What they keep saying is an unprovable assumption but with the general public being so ignorant on how a free market place actually works it allows the liberals to keep running their phony shell game. All of that money was actually wasted and did far more damage to the economy.

Proof of why it actually did more

damage than good is what it did to government. The sound free market place formula is very simple, more and bigger government is bad because that means government must take even more of the dwindling profit businesses are struggling to survive on.

It not only took the nation trillions deeper into debt it vastly increased the growth in government which makes the nation and the economy far worse off than before the stimulus.

The fact is more and bigger government is bad, and smaller and lesser government is good if this nation is to survive, but, of course, trying to get a shallow minded liberal to understand something so simple is a horse of a different color.

So, the real proof is instead of the stimulus package saving the USA economy it stepped up the pace of the slow death watch we are on. The day of reckoning looms on the horizon. Like a broken record I must throw this in, the elimination of the minimum wage will force this nation to save itself, there is no other option.

My great wisdom and destiny demands I keep sounding my same stress call "The elimination of the minimum wage is a must, period," with love always.
SIRMANS LOG: 17 FEBRUARY 2012, 1854 HOURS

LESSER OF TWO EVILS AND LIKING IT!
I am not a scheming or devious type person and don't think in those terms, but, there are some who do and is very good at it. In politics there is a very old tactic and I think Richard M. Nixon honed it almost to a science with submitting Supreme Court justices.

First you trot out someone or something extreme that you know probably won't be accepted, then when the noise die down you ease in your real intent and it will be gladly

accepted. Just a little food for thought, that is all, good day.
SIRMANS LOG: 12 FEBRUARY 2012, 1700 HOURS.

CURRENT EVENT INJECTION 19 JANUARY 2012:
KEYSTONE OIL PIPELINE DECISION!
I definitely don't need this, I would be far better off keeping my personal view to my self on this matter, but, I guess I'm a motor mouth at times and can't help it.

Anyone that has ever read any of my writing knows that I'm for small government and totally against a welfare state type government. That means that I disagree almost one hundred percent of the time with the current administrations policies. But, on this Keystone Pipeline issue I must admit that I totally agree with their decision on this.

Experts have been wrong before and will be wrong again, that is a given. Why take a chance and risk destroying the water supply of three states when it can be avoided. Sure, the cost is going to be much higher and take longer, but later saying that shouldn't have happen, or saying we are sorry won't bring back clean water.

I have personally experienced Murphy's Law in action many times. Murphy's Law says if anything bad can possibly happen it will. I think the risk is just far too great no matter what the experts say when you are talking about the water supply of three states.

To me it is a no brainier, just go around the aquifer. Sure, we are desperate in need of jobs but first we must have clean water to live.

CURRENT EVENT INJECTION 19 JANUARY 2012:
WHAT A DREAM TEAM?
Newt + JC

CURRENT EVENT INJECTION 16 JANUARY 2012!
THE CRUISE LINE INCIDENT:
MY BIGGEST SURPRISE AND MAYBE A BIGGER QUESTION IS:
Why would a modern ship like that go down so fast? I thought in modern ship building at least some type of compartmentalized structure would be in place, but, again what do I know, maybe it is too cost prohibitive. No matter how well trained the crew, a ship going down that fast with that many people there are going to be problems.

DISSECTING USA ECONOMY
Like I've said many times, I can dissect an economy as well as anyone.
Here is my bold brash opinion on the options if the USA and western civilization is to survive.

The way I see the situation in the USA is first things first and I've yet to hear anyone hit the target. To talk about getting out of debt or saving our freedom while government is still in the role of super social and family provider in my view is dumb and stupid.

That is something that is impossible, we are lucky that this has lasted this long. You see, government doesn't have any money and every penny it takes comes from some type of business profit. The bigger government gets the more profit it must take from businesses until it kills off all business profit. We are not there yet, but we are headed there at warp speed.

Sure, government taxes the people and almost everything else that exist, but where do the people get there money, ultimately like I said all income leads back to some type of business transaction.

A society must have some type of government for internal and external protection of the whole society otherwise government wouldn't be needed. Government is not part of an economy it is just a parasite

needed for protection. In simple terms, an economy consists of only
two players, a seller and a buyer no matter how modern or complicated
it may seem.

Starting with the seller, using some form of energy the seller produces a product or service and a buyer purchases it. An employee himself is actually a seller, he sell his labor for a paycheck. A business itself is only a medium of exchange to generate a profit for the owner, if it doesn't generate a profit it can't exist.

To sum it up, government is only needed to protect society, but, it has the big guns and the power to take over and some do. And believe it or not with the course we are on that is exactly what is going to happen to the great USA, it is only logic.

Unless we start by eliminating the minimum wage and void practically all regulations the economy is guaranteed to totally collapse. After that there will be mass hunger, rioting in the streets and a lot of people being shot, then the people themselves will demand that government take over.

However, with the eliminating of the minimum wage and choking regulations government won't collapse, but it will severely deflate and a lot of rich people will go broke. But, we will save out freedom and survive, it won't be easy but the people will regain control and the nation will survive.

Otherwise, with the course we are on freedom and the nation will be lost forever. There it is y'all all wrapped and packaged, you don't have to agree with me but that is my brief analysis.

Sure, government shouldn't be in the role of super social and family provider, but, when all else has failed government does has a responsibility to not let the poor freeze or starve. However, government also should never hand out free unearned money or food stamps to the poor or anyone else if the free market place is to survive.

The only way government can help the poor without destroying the nuclear family, the culture, and the economy is to establish government runs commissaries, housing, and clinics with the use of tokens or script for those who qualify.

Government handing out free cash and food stamps guarantees a big enough pool of paying customers where the merchant don't ever have to lower prices, thereby causing higher prices and taxes on everyone.
That is what's causing this out of control consumer inflation that is killing us today.

Government can spend all it wants to and it won't cause consumer inflation unless money is handed out on an individual basis, the individual basis is what destroys the natural balance between the buyer and the seller.

I will tell any conservative, okay, you want small government, well; you can't get there from here. First, where you start is fight to eliminate the minimum wage and void countless choking regulations that will get you there, there is no other way, period.
SIRMANS LOG: 10 JANUARY 1727, 1005 HOURS

In sheer economic terms government as a social and family provider and having a lasting free market place at the same time simply don't mix, it is like pouring water in acid. It not only destroys a free market place economy it corrupts morals and leaves a nations culture in total ruins.

Look what the welfare state has done to the great USA, we are totally broke with trillions of dollars in debt which makes us slaves to foreign sources. And what is even scarier is we have a shallow hype prone predominate liberal news media that has left the general public totally in the dark on the true state of the nation.

With little to no nuclear and extended family foundation left and any minimum bartering capacity to sustain us under distress, this nation could become authoritarian or a dictatorship almost overnight.

In my opinion with the czars already in place and with a shallow predominate liberal news media that can't recognize a moral or deep threat if it slapped them upside the head, the only thing now saving the last bastion of true freedom in the world today is the second amendment. And its days are probably numbered.

All of which could be avoided if the minimum wage was eliminated and all big government regulations were voided and then added back as needed. We as a nation are like fools with all of our eggs still in one giant big government welfare state basket, how sad, God help us.

Around the world I imagine many are amused by the fix we are in. But, at the same time they are in almost boot shaking fear, because wise men know the most dangerous thing there is, is when a great nation is injured or losing power.
05 JANUARY 2012, NEW INJECTION:

<u>My God! Maybe my deep wisdom is greater than even I realize.</u> Things about the economy that seems so simple to me doesn't even register with the so called highly intelligent great economic thinkers of today.

I listen every day on this and that and what this politician is going to do to fix the economy and on and on. While at the same time welfare states all over the world is in the early stages of collapsing down upon their heads.

Still, the powers that be don't even have a clue as to the one and only thing that can save the USA and western civilization. I believe the global economy is past the stage of no return, it can't be saved, but at least western civilization itself can be saved if this one and only thing is done.

The one and only thing that I know without a shadow of doubt that will save western civilization is "Get government out of the role of social and family provider, period." However, after eighty years of ever increasing big government dependency that is an almost impossible task.

Also, another go against the grain widely held false assumption that flies in the face of sound economics is the belief that the "Minimum wage is a good thing." In economic terms the minimum wage is destructive wishful thinking, period. The minimum wage doesn't increase wealth it only distorts wealth and kills the free market place.

The minimum wage makes what cost $5.00 after awhile cost $50.00. The only thing that increases wealth is the increase in production and buying power. Without the elimination of the minimum wage it will be impossible to get the government out of its family provider role to save western civilization.

Power will always go down with the ship, only divine intervention can save us now, God help us. Government in the role of social and family provider given time will always kill an economy. It is done by taking too much profit leaving no incentive for anyone to go into or stay in business.

Given time big government will also snuff out all greed and self-interest which leaves no incentive to produce except by the whip. With the whip one will produce only enough to stay alive which is the history of communism and socialism.

So, there it is in a nut shell folks, you have the facts and a solution. You can dismiss me, the facts, and everything else I say, but you won't

prove me wrong.
SIRMANS LOG: 04 JANUARY 2012, 1220 HOURS

CURRENT EVENT INJECTION!
THE PAYROLL TAX CUT EXTENSION: Some people are coming down hard on the house speaker saying he is a caver and can't stand up to pressure. Well, I for one totally disagree; I think he made the right decision on avoiding a tax raise on the American people.

Sure, the liberals are demagoguing the issue but that is expected and beside the point. You have a general public that is 95 percent ignorant on economic matters, they can't see past their noses and will be film flamed almost every time by the liberals, what is one to do.

With the liberals and their cohorts in

the new media pouring on the
demagoguery there is no doubt who
will get the blame. Educating the
public is the only real solution but that
is no easy task after eighty years
of big government liberal do-for-me
entitlement propaganda.

Facing unreasonable odds a wise man
will try to live to fight another
day hopefully on terms more to his
favor. "Fools rush in where wise
men fear to tread."
SIRMANS LOG: 24 DECEMBER 2011,
0055 HOURS

WITH NO MINIMUM WAGE THE RICH
HAS THE MOST TO LOSE THE POOR IS
ALREADY DIRT POOR!
Here is the skinny on this minimum
wage thing I keep harping on. Sure,
I know almost everybody is thinking
that I'm a fool and don't know
what the hell I'm talking about, and
besides, they feel it will never
happen anyway. And they are probably
right because I have no power
to make anyone do anything.

Plus, everybody keep thinking that it
don't make sense because the
poor can't make it as is, they need to
raise the minimum wage not get
rid of it. Wrong, wrong, wrong, it is
just the opposite and I so happen to
be one of the very few with the
wisdom and perspective to see it.

Without the minimum wage the
welfare state beast will get starved out
of its cradle to grave super provider
role. Without government driving
up and keeping prices high by giving
money and food stamps to the
poor it would be impossible for prices
to go above what the poor can
afford because there is never enough
rich to keep commerce flowing.

Sure, government must help the very
poor and not let people starve but
it can be done without destroying our
culture and economy like what
the welfare state has done. The way
you help the poor and not destroy
the culture, the economy, freedom,
and everything else is by

establishing government run commissaries, housing, and clinics.

Plus, tokens or script must be issued to those that qualify to keep from contaminating the national free market place currency. The reason for that is there are only two players in an economy they are the <u>seller and buyer</u>, or the <u>merchant and consumer</u>.

Government was created to guard and protect the process plus the whole society. However, government has the big guns and the fighters, so, without an armed populace it is a lot easier for a tyrant to try to seize power and take over.

Through natures supreme law of "Natural selection" the <u>buyer and seller</u> will always keep a natural balance between the two. But, when government put in a minimum wage and all kind of regulations it destroys the balance between the <u>buyer</u> and the <u>seller</u>.

The government creates consumer

inflation by giving enough <u>buyers</u> (poor) the money to afford super high prices. The <u>merchant</u> then get away with raising prices because government is paying a large enough pool to allow it, otherwise prices would have to remain lower enough for most poor folks to pay their own doctor and food bills.

Once government got a taste of being a provider it got drunk on the control and power of lording it over people. So, it decide to create the great society, food stamps and everything else from cradle to grave, no problem, just raise taxes a little higher.

While all of this was going on the rich and the very poor had it made while consumer inflation was eating the middle class alive. To tell the truth folks, I don't know how things will finally play out if the minimum is eliminated. But, I do know that if it is not eliminated we will lose our freedom and maybe even our country.

USA ECONOMY FIXING TO CRASH, BRACE FOR IMPACT!

I don't have to be right and no one may agree with anything I write, still, this is the way I see it.
SIRMANS LOG: 17 DECEMBER 2011, 0014 HOURS

WHY THE POOR CAN'T CREATE SOME OF THEIR OWN JOBS

OK, OK, I hear you America! This is what big government and the welfare state has brought us to. I think the nation is at death door and its going to come down to first just eating and surviving. I think it is better to eat and survive than to have untold amounts of gold and riches and starve.

Once there is no threat of starving then the sky can be the limit. I'm going to go out on a limb and say something that is taboo and political incorrect way beyond measure. I'm saying there is a place for "Roles" in life provided they are not set in stone and there is freedom of choice.

Throughout history until the "New

deal" and the welfare state the children, the sick, and the elderly were always taken care of in a healthy and stable environment. To me it is a given the welfare state is now collapsing down upon us I see it and know it but the egg heads and elites will never admit it until it is too late.

So, what are we going to do about being prepared when we know a change is gonna come. I think its going to come down to bare bone survival I'm here to tell you with a minimum wage in place we have absolutely no chance of surviving.

There will be millions upon million starving to death and it could take civilization back to the Stone Age. The minimum wage and government regulations are blocking anyone from bartering and surviving on their own.

No one will escape and no amount of wealth is going to get you food if no one is willing to sell. Even if you have prepared and have food it would take an army to protect you with millions starving around you.

It is simple if there was no minimum wage at least the people could barter and do for each other just to eat if nothing more. But, with a minimum wage and countless big government regulations blocking you at every turn no amount of self-initiative is gonna keep you from starving.

As it is now the welfare state as a super family provider has nearly destroyed what has guaranteed human survival for over 5,000 years, the nuclear and extended family and its "Role" system.

Sure, opportunity and freedom to all is a must and no one doubts that in this great nation. But, who is going to raise the children and care for the sick and elderly when soon our big government will be totally broke with no borrowing power.

I'm telling you its not gong to get

better like the egg heads and the elites keep promising, mass starvation is on its way whether we like it or not. I'm telling you we are about to face the sheer survival of the USA and western civilization itself.

I feel it is my destiny at all cost to get out the stress call for this nations survival no matter my handicaps and flaws. Agree or not I feel it is a calling and duty. I fear and hate the limelight. I also feel the minimum wage is standing in the way of this nation's survival.

All praise be to God. We shall survive. Minimum wage "I banish you" in the name of God.
SIRMANS LOG: 15 DECEMBER 2011, 0123 HOURS

SLAVERY IN ECONOMIC TERMS!
Slavery is still around in some isolated cases. When you go back in history before western civilization and private land ownership slavery played a major role in economics.

I keep telling people a free market place with free competition is the only way a nation can feed all of its people. In economic terms what freedom and the free market place actually do is release two of the most energizing forces in our human makeup.

Even today very few American understand these two forces especially liberals because on the surface they seem to go against the grain of the status quo. If you lack wisdom and perspective you won't understand these two forces which is the case with the vast majority of Americans.

The two forces I'm talking about are greed and self-interest. Like electricity these two forces are dangerous and can be deadly. The key is
to harness these two powerful forces but never shut them down or
hinder them too much. Only a free market place will harness this super powerful energy in a way that will

produce almost unlimited abundance in everything.

Anybody following Keynesian Theory don't know what the hell is going on in this day and time in my view. I can dissect an economy myself, and there is no doubt in my mind the welfare state cannot and will not survive, period.

Except for a free market place economy every other economic system tends to hinder or shutoff greed and self-interest. I predict within five years the world is going to experience slavery and starving in a major way. There is nothing complicated about it, it is simply human nature at work.

No one is going to be caring and do extra work when some one else is doing less and receiving an equal reward. Sure, using fear and pain will get some production but never an abundance. In this nuclear weapon age no powerful nation can get away with taking over smaller weaker nations and working them like slaves like in the distance past.

So, without a true free market place economy I will guarantee you slavery will be back with a vengeance. With no one being able to make a profit due to big government there simply will be no other way for a nation to survive. I tell it as I see it. Praise be to God, Hallelujah.
SIRMANS LOG: 11 DECEMBER 2011, 12 MIDNIGHT.
PS: The biggest problem with the USA is we have gotten too far away from a true free market place economy. It is impossible to have a true free market place economy with a minimum wage in place.

UNITED STATES POST OFFICE DEBACLE?
I have my own take on the U.S. Postal Service debacle and decided to weigh in on this matter. I can only give my one man opinion on what I think is going on. It may be sort of like social security with government

siphoning off money for other government spending.

My belief is some of the money that should be going to the Postal service is probably being secretly siphoned off for other government spending. Unlike most government agencies the United States Postal service is a fee for service agency.

That being the case by all means the Postal service should be able to stand on its own. I think there is a lot more going on with the Postal Service than meets the eye. The first thing is I believe there are too many cooks in the management kitchen.

The second thing is I believe politics has a strangle hold on management with no one with any real power in charge of running the place. Sure, the unions are a factor and play a major role, still, with long term low interest loans there is no logical reason why the Postal Service can't survive without all of these cutbacks.

Come on! Give me a break! Like I said, I believe somewhere money is being siphoned off and spent elsewhere in the government; however, there is no way for me to prove that.
SIRMANS LOG: 7 DECEMBER 2011, 2148 HOURS

BOLD AND IN YOUR FACE!
In my view "The Bloom is off the rose, the cat is out of the bag," the progressive liberals are throwing rocks as always but now no longer feel a need to hide their hand anymore.

We can now see from top to bottom that the progressive liberals are openly promoting the "All for one and one for all" socialist and centralized communist like thinking. To them Individual freedom, small government, and a free market place all are seen as "The enemy of the people."

Plus, with a shallow economically ignorant predominate liberal news media riding shotgun they no longer feel a need to hide their real intent anymore. And with eighty years of false you-owe-me liberal entitlement mentality indoctrination they just may be right.

God I ask in your name, save the great USA.
SIRMANS LOG: 7 DECEMBER 2011, 0951 HOURS
PS: And another thing, I think giving the military the power to arrest civilians is a first step toward taking our guns away.

Sure, the liberals played the biggest role in birthing our welfare state.
But, this nation didn't get on the brink of a total economic collapse with just liberals; a lot of conservatives took the course of least resistance
and looked the other way.

We know as a rule liberals are basically shallow and live in the moment, but what can be just as dangerous to freedom is a shallow conservative, especially if he want to give arresting power to the military to arrest civilians.

JUST A LITTLE INJECTION CONCERNING "PROFIT."

I have never considered myself to be an exceptional intelligent person, still, for the life of me I can't understand why I can dissect an economy
so clearly while ninety five percent of the USA population just don't get it.

To understand economics all you need to do is understand one thing and that will be ninety five percent of the battle. That one thing is profit, profit, profit, and more profit. If you don't understand what profit is you are lost and don't know what wealth is either.

I will give a quick walk through background. In the beginning before the proper tools and weapons man spent most of his awake time hunting and searching for food. There

was no profit because profit is
the ability to have more than you need
to live on.

Once farming reach the stage to store
grain and domesticate animals
then profit could be realized as long as
one had enough for himself and
family to get through the winter. Plus,
seed stock and seed grain had to
be maintained, then whatever one had
over that was called profit. So, in
the final analysis it will always boil
down to eating or starving.

You can't eat money or any material
possession. All this big government
and welfare state stuff ain't gonna feed
nobody if not enough people are
producing food. Why go into business
when all your profit goes to someone
else, it's not quite there yet, but it is
getting harder and harder for any
business to make a profit.

That's the problem with liberals, they
don't give a damn what they destroy
as long as they stay in power. But, in
the end there will be no power to be

had because there will not be anyone making any profit for government to take and survive on

Get a grip America! One hundred years ago the only place you could find a liberal was in a rich family or maybe on a college campus. Now, the welfare state has made practical all of the poor hardcore liberals.

In over 5,000 years of written history when has the very poor ever been in favor of killing babies in the womb and men marring men, give me a break, people. And I'm supposed to be the nut case, here. I, Freddie L. Sirmans Senior will not shut up and look the other way.
SIRMANS LOG: 2 DECEMBER 2011, 2355 HOURS

IT'S TIME FOR SOME FORM OF LEGAL PROSTITUTION TO GET CONTROL OVER PORN IF NOTHING ELSE! I HAD GRAVE RESERVATIONS ABOUT ADDING THIS ARTICLE BUT DECIDED TO DO IT ANYWAY COMES WHAT MAY.

THIS IS MY ONE MANS OPINIONS ON WHY I THINK PORN IS TOTALLY OUT OF CONTROL. VERY FEW AGREE WITH ME, BUT I STAND BY MY REASONING ON THIS.

LOOK AT WHAT IS HAPPENING TO SOME OF THE SOCIAL WEBSITES AND THE PERVERTED SEXUAL SMUT THAT MANY YOUNG KIDS HAVE TO WITNESS. I'M POWERLESS TO STOP ANYTHING BUT I WANT EVERYONE TO KNOW THAT I'M MORALLY AGAINST ALL THIS MORAL ROT AND DECAY.

JUST LIKE EVERYTHING ELSE MONEY AND PAYING CUSTOMERS IS WHAT DRIVES THE PORN INDUSTRY.
SIRMANS LOG: 16 NOVEMBER 2011, 2357 HOURS

OHIO VOTE EQUALS MOB RULE ECONOMICALLY WISE!
"We have a republic if we can keep it." The founding fathers almost to a man believed that pure democracy was nothing more than mob rule, that is why we actually have a republic form

of government.

The general public as a whole is almost always ignorant and uninformed on how to run a working government. It takes strong leadership that will proper educate the public and bring them along to have and keep a successful government in a free society.

Overall, I don't blame the citizens for what happened in Ohio. But, I do blame the progressive liberals that used the depression to seize the family provider role for itself and birthed the welfare state we have today. And as long as our government is in the provider role nothing or no one is going to stop it from taking the last red cent from anyone that makes a profit.

Riding shotgun for the progressive liberals are the vast predominate liberal news media which has educated to some degree 95 percent of the general public with this false welfare state you-owe-me entitlement mentality.

I'm here to tell you, you can't get blood out of a turnip meaning because of too high taxes soon no one will be able to make a profit, then guess what, there will be no one making any profit for government to take in the form of taxes. Then a broke government ain't gonna be taking care of anyone. The people are supposed to be taking care of the government not the government taking care of the people in the first place.

The nuclear and extended family system have never failed to guarantee human survival in well over 5,000 years. But, here we are with our dumb asses putting all of our faith in a welfare state beast that dies with a broke government. And there has never been and never will be a government that doesn't go broke at some point. Also, according to the supreme law of nature when you take away the survival need for anything you make it extinct in time.

With the welfare state that is what we are doing to the nuclear and extended family system by slowly making it extinct. There must be a divine reason why a neurotic handicap like me came out of the woodworks to bring back some sanity before all of this shallow dumb insane thinking takes this great nation over a cliff.

Sure, the Ohio voters won their public employees union battle, but that will demand higher taxes. The unions may have won that battle but the whole state will loose the war when people begin starving.

Sure, the Ohio voters won their public employees union battle, but that will demand higher taxes. The unions may have won that battle but the whole state will loose the war when people begin starving.

When you kill the goose that lays the golden egg of profit with the scatter gun of higher and higher taxes, mass starvation always follow. Nature's supreme law of "Natural selection" guarantees that. And the reason we have never ending higher and higher taxes is because government is a family provider.

Sure, veteran and a few other pensioners are a good thing, but government should never become a mass family provider if it is to survive long term, because like any broke and desperate family provider it's going to lie, beg, borrow, or steal to feed its dependents.
So, if you think our soon to be broke provider welfare state won't do something terrible and unimaginable you are fooling yourself.

However, government does have a duty as a last resort to make sure the poor and needy doesn't freeze or starve. But, the only way the government can help the poor and needy without destroying the free market place economy is to establish government run commissaries, housing, and clinics. And token or script must be used to prevent contamination of the nations currency.

Government should never under any condition give out free money or food stamps on an individual basis. The key is "Individual basis," because that act alone is what ignites consumer inflation by creating a bigger enough pool to allow high priced merchants to never have to lower their prices in order to stay in business.

That causes everyone to pay higher and higher prices and taxes in a never ending upward spiral, and it also destroys the buying power of the dollar in the process. No matter what the learned egg heads and elites may tell you, "I" say nothing else can ignite and driver consumer inflation out of sight like what is happening now, I double dog dare you , prove me wrong.

See my emergency USA survival blueprint > http://www.flsirmans.com/FLSirmansEmergencyUSAsurvivalBluePrint
SIRMANS LOG: 9 NOVEMBER 2011,

1815 HOURS

THE PHENOMENON OF "HERMAN CAIN" AS SEEN BY SELF-MADE WRITER FREDDIE L. SIRMANS, SR.
They say that life is a cycle and history repeats itself. And in this case we may again have two great African American men squaring off to shape the course of history, but in this case it is not about their race but the direction of the whole nation.

In the first case it was William E. B. Du Bois versus Booker T. Washington on which course the African American race would take. Washington believed that African Americans should take the self reliance route and focus first on learning the basic trade vocations to feed and control their own destiny.

He didn't put a priority on integration. On the other hand, Du bois disagreed openly in public with Washington and believed that African Americans should not be limited in anyway. Du bois believed that blacks should go the full integration route and focus on the best education possibly.

Du bois way won out on the course blacks should take. Sure, overall Du Bois way did win out in theory but it have never paned out in practice even to this day in my view.

However, this time around so much about America has greatly changed; African Americans are no longer the largest minority group anymore. Plus, in my view the ideology factor is even more the deciding factor than the race factor except for the fewer and fewer secret raciest.

In my view and backed by what I seen on a call in TV show, most of the most vicious attacks on Cain came from African American callers, even one black lady called him a monkey. Coming out of slavery and even to this day I don't think most African Americans have unconditional accepted a black identity.

I think still far too many African Americans see other blacks as competitors and in some cases the enemy instead of an honorable fellow independent authority figure. Why else would so many of us use the hated "N" word in private if not in public as if it doesn't apply to each of us personally.

I think the welfare state has locked most African Americans into a do-for-me dependent mode. I think one political party practical own the African American race, and that could never happen to a people that individually think for themselves.

That said, enough of me putting down my proud African American race. No one, no race, and no nation is perfect. When all is said and done, overall I truly believe the African American race to be one of the greatest people to ever exist. Sure, I may criticize and come down hard, but to me it is constructive criticism and done out of genuine love.

Against overwhelming odds and stripped of their culture, language, and religion these people withstood slavery and came out illiterate in a hostile environment with almost nothing. They didn't have the option to escape and blend in because of their color.

Still, they created Jazz, and have made great achievements in every phase of American life, they are survivors. And today we see a man of color in the White house, and even greater is a country that have allow this unlimited freedom to happen.

At heart I'm a conservative, but in practice I behave more as a pragmatist or realist. A black conservative to a liberal is like someone shelving a Christian cross in the face of vampire. They screech and see it as a threat to their very being, and that same reaction also applies to the hordes of dependents depending on the liberals to stay in power.

The mass liberal media will never accept a genuine African American conservative in my view. They just can't understand why a black person in their view can reject their helpful do-good intentions. You see, it is all about control to them, a liberal loves controlling more than anything else because that adds a purpose to their life.

A self-sufficient do-for-yourself conservative black threatens the whole welfare state reason for being, and to a liberal there is no greater sin.
To them he must be destroyed at all cost.

Which way will the nation go? Will it zoom warp speed into a failed socialist European like system or take the small government free market place course as the founding fathers designed the country to be, your vote matters, the future is in our hands.

PS: 2 NOVEMBER 2011, 0106 HOURS: BRIEF INJECTION:
I may be wrong on this, but if anything can pry the 90 percent plus loose this

may be it the way the vicious partisan liberal media are going after this decent high moral black man.
SIRMANS LOG: 30 OCTOBER 2011, 1343 HOURS

SIRMANS LOG: 4 DECEMBER 2011, 1745 HOURS
Well, Herman Cain decided to throw in the towel, who can blame him. That means there won't be a showdown between two men of color for the president of the United States.

I think Dick Nixon said it best when he said "You won't have Richard Nixon to kick around anymore." Well, in my view the bias predominate liberal news media won't have "Ole Herman" to kick around anymore.

PS: Here is the reason for the 90 percent plus African American voting for one political party in every election in my view

I DON'T KNOW WHEN, BUT I KNOW THE USA ECONOMY IS GOING TO

COLLAPSE. I AM SO PROUD TO BE AN AMERICAN, FOR SOME STRANGE REASON I JUST FELT A NEED TO SAY THAT.

When I promise you the USA economy is going to collapse it really is a no brainier because it is the same as saying everybody is going to die. I understand it but the egg heads and the elites have tunnel vision and don't understand the role nature plays in economics.

Mother natures supreme law of "Natural selection" controls economics and everything else that exist. According to the law of natural selection there must be a survival need for anything to continue to exist, otherwise nature starts getting rid of it.

There is no survival need for moral decay and inefficiency, so it gotta go and if it means taking down a nation, too bad. Everything erodes or decays in some way and that includes ideas. Look at the great USA; it is now weighted down with moral decay, big government waste and inefficiency.

But, big government is much too powerful and will never allow small correcting purges that would cause much hardship but save the national economy. That is why nature's law of natural selection has no choice but to take down the nation's economy and maybe the whole world economy.

However, nothing in the future is ever written in stone man through his actions always has the power to determine his destiny. Throughout history there has never been a nation that changed course knowing it was headed toward disaster.

The reason is power never willingly concedes an inch, those wielding power will always go down with the ship. Due to the Rosetta stone we know that a written history and civilization goes back well over 5,000 years. The Roman Empire lasted a thousand years.

Ever since the dawn of history governments and rulers have always come and go, but, there was three constants over time that always stood firm until the "New deal" birthed the welfare state. Now, the whole of western civilization is on the ropes and may not survive all due to the infestation of the welfare state.

The three constants I'm talking about are the three pillars that allows human civilization to exist in my view: (1) A strong nuclear and extended family system, (2) a strong moral and religious code, (3) and adequate emergency bartering capacity with many, many small farmer and home gardeners in case the economy collapses.

Since the "New deal" birthed our welfare state we now depend almost entirely on our super provider welfare state from cradle to grave. Neglecting and dismissing the things that has safeguarded civilization

for over 5,000 years to me is pass dumb and stupid, it is sheer madness. God forgive us.
SIRMANS LOG: 24 OCTOBER 2011, 2247 HOURS.

MY ANALYSIS ON WALL STREET OCCUPIERS!
I believe what you see being played out with the Wall Street occupiers is a microcosmic example of what is being learned on the nation's universities and college's campuses.

I think almost 95 percent of the American people to some extent have bought into the liberal welfare state entitlement mentality. They call it the safety net and feeding the welfare state beast must be done to protect that at all cost.

This nation has been around 235 years and has always had to struggle with financial ups and downs but it was always armed with a strong nuclear and extended family system along with a good moral and religious code in place.

Starting with the "New deal" that birthed our welfare state we no longer have these solid foundation building blocks to withstand an all out struggle to survive as a free nation any more. Sure, we can keep feeding our tax hungry welfare state beast a little longer to buy time, but unless my blue print survival plan is taken seriously I see very little hope. See my emergency USA survival blueprint > http://www.flsirmans.com/FLSirmansEmergencyUSAsurvivalBluePrint

I believe what you see with the Wall Street occupiers are people with very weak survival instincts that have bought the liberal claptrap welfare state entitlement mentality lock stock and barrel. They don't care or even realize that with very few exceptions the rich got their money the hard way, they worked for it and made great sacrifices.

They don't realize that job don't just

drop out of heaven. They don't realize that jobs are created by people just like you and I that didn't sit around waiting on someone else to act. These people took great financial risk and in most cases fought against great odds to provide a job for themselves and many, many others.

These people are our job providers and should be praised. And anyone attacking them is either ignorant or stupid in my view. Even the definition of what a job is has been distorted. Everybody is all hung up on thinking that a job must come with health and pension benefits, nonsense, that is something that started with our welfare state.

Sure, to get that is great but to get any job to survive should be the first priority. Myself, I blame everything that is causing our downfall on our welfare state. Today even someone with self-initiative have a mountain to climb because of all kind of government licenses and permits.

It is getting to where it is almost impossible for some one to start small. Starting small is what made America great? The old saying "Living of the land doesn't apply anymore. I don't know where it is all going to end, but, I do know without a doubt that our welfare state cannot and will not survive. God save America.
SIRMANS LOG: 23 OCTOBER 2011, 0104 HOURS

PS: And here is another thing I decided to comment on. But, let me say this first, I seldom comment on any politician or any individual. Here goes my take on governor Perry, I don't care what anyone says I believe it is what he said about social security that have hurt his chances to be president.

I, and many, many others totally agree that what he said was factual true, but we are not trying to become president of the united states. I remember when he first entered the race and zoomed right to the top.

I, like most Americans knew only that he was a very successful Texas governor.

I have heard the old folks mention first impressions many times, but even now I never get carried away on something like that, the same as judging a book by the cover, but I guess in some cases it really does matter.

Right after he called social security a ponzi scheme I thought to myself, wow, does he know the old folks are the biggest and most powerful voting block in the country, and social security is like a God to them? So, in my view that statement was like spotting your opponent twenty paces from git go.

Sure, the pundits will be all over the map with all kinds of reasons why he can't get a leg up, but I believe unless he can find a way to defuse that social security statement nothing is going to work. There is no running away from it he must go for an all out repent of his sin and ask for complete forgiveness for speaking ill will against social security.

He must promise to never attack or speak ill will of social security ever again. Nothing short of getting the old folks to forgive him of his past social security beliefs are going to allow him to become president of these United States in my view.

There is no shame in just saying I was just plain wrong about social security, the old folks are a caring and forgiving people. Besides, there was one powerful bible character that spent years putting down Christianity but ended up being one of its greatest protectors.

I, Freddie L. Sirmans, Sr. I am a self-made writer that write what I truly think and believe, I could be wrong on this but that is my analysis.

EVERYBODY IS ALREADY PAYING TOO MUCH TAX, AND DEMONIZING THE

RICH IS STUPID IN MY VIEW!
"GOOD GOVERNMENT IS A
PROTECTOR NOT A PROVIDER!"
I found myself smiling while listening
to a liberal lion go on and on about
the rich not paying their fair share of
taxes and blaming everything on
the republicans.

Whereas, I know beyond a shadow of a
doubt that it is the liberals
claptrap garbage mentality that have
brought this great country almost
to its knees with this welfare state
beast Lording it over all of us. The
reason why I couldn't help but smile is
because sometimes humor is the
best way to defuse and accept a sad
situation.

As I sat listening to this super liberal
lion spout on and on the standard
liberal blame shifting garbage it made
me feel so befuddled and sad
knowing nearly half of the nation is
flimflammed by this stuff. I'm afraid
it may be too late now history and our
destruction is on the liberals side
unless a miracle take place, its going

to take some hard decisions and
hardship to save this nation and I'm
not for sure we have the stomach
for it.

I am almost alone yelling and hollering
to deaf ears, no one want to hear
me, when I yell get rid of the minimum
wage and never give anyone
money or food stamps on an individual
basis, they think my God give
wisdom is stupid. Still, I will never
loose hope and stop trying to help
save this great nation.

Like I have said many times before
when it becomes almost totally
acceptable to attack the rich, freedom
and democracy is on its last leg,
and I condemn anyone that does it.
When you see entertainers, sport
figures, business executives and others
making extreme amounts of
money that is because of big
government and our welfare state,
don't blame these people more power
to them.

In a free market place economy with

unhindered competition no
extremes can get out of hand, only
government can get between the
merchant and the consumer and ignite
consumer inflation by subsiding
higher and higher prices enabling
enough people to pay them. There
never has been and never will be a rich
and prosperous country without
a lot of rich people to make it happen.

Poor people with money are not the
same as rich people, there is a world
of difference in mentality, plus almost
all rich people have a strong
sense of altruism, which is not the case
with most of the very, very poor.
It may not seem so, but if you scratch
below the surface of most
genuine failures in life you will find a
very self centered individual.

Without exceptions trying to make
everyone equal in life will always
make everyone equally poor except a
very few privileged leaders. Look
at history, the first thing every dictator
or any power grabber does is go
after and attack the rich, because they

know the rich is the lifeblood of every democracy.

In a democracy the loyalty of the rich is a must because if the rich can't keep and hold on to their money they have the means to leave. I believe turning people against the rich is one of the most destructive things you can do to a free and democratic country. The old saying "Ways and actions speak louder than words" should wake people up but it doesn't.

Myself, I have been out here for years beating the bushes trying to drive the political snakes out into the opening, but to little or no avail. I think the liberals really mean well but human beings and what motivates them is something they have never understood.

Liberals just don't care or understand that when you do for and make a human being a dependent you destroy that persons will to survive on his own. Balance is the real key to human survival, to little struggle to survive can be as bad as too much hardship to survive.

One reason why we may loose our freedom is our lack of instilling good judgment and character in our young. I believe good sound judgment and character can only be instilled with a certain amount of real or imposed hardship and struggle. I'm not in favor of any harsh extreme hazing, but the idea comes from imposing some form of hardship to help build character.

Sure, many will disagree with me on the necessity of hardship and struggle to build character; still I stand my ground on this. Why do you think drug use is so out of control in this country, character may not be the main factor but it definitely plays a role?

The struggle to survive in all species have evolved over thousands of years and when struggle is taken away life tends to become less appreciated and leaves an unfulfilled void. To a large extent that is what has happen to this great country, far too many people today have weak survival instincts.

Far too many people couldn't recognize a moral threat if it slapped them upside the head. Far too many feel, who care if a man marries a man or a woman, marries a woman. Far too many feel it is only a fetus, who cares; the welfare state is going to take care of me in my old age.

What they don't know is nothing or no one escapes nature's supreme law of "Natural selection" but only so long. Nature's supreme law of natural selection purges out moral decay, inefficiency, and waste through births and rebirths.

The world is entering the early stage of a rebirth, and I'm here to tell you any nation without a strong nuclear and extended family system, a strong moral and religious code, and some bartering capacity with small farmers and home gardeners will have

little or no chance of surviving.
SIRMANS LOG: 17 OCTOBER 2011,
2045 HOURS.

EMERGENCY USA SURVIVAL BLUE PRINT.
I stump my shoe hard on the wood floor and slam my hat down on the floor, too! And think, damn, damn, damn! Can't somebody understand simple logic! I'm no genus, what I keep telling people is just simple logic, whatever happened to people with even a little perspective! Have the welfare state destroyed even that!

Here it is again in a nut shell, I'm talking about the core problem, the root problem, the heart of the matter, the eye of the storm or whatever you call it. No amount of money or anything you do is going to save the USA and our freedom as long as we have a super family provider welfare state beast in control.

Nothing and I mean nothing as long as government is giving out money

and food stamps on an individual basis is going to save our economy
simply because that act alone kills the free market and drives inflation.
So, until the government is out of the family provider role 9-9-9 or any revenue raising or anything else is going to saving our great nation.

A provider welfare state is like a giant snowball rolling down hill,
nothing is going to stop it. The more it takes in taxes the more it's going to need to feed its growing list of dependents, it feeds on itself, the more it grows the more it demands in never ending new taxes. Look what it has already done to the great USA, It has already almost totally destroyed the African American nuclear family and the rest of the country is not too far behind.

It has ripped our morals to threads where the word marriage now means anything one want it to. And our culture has come to mean me first, I want mine, I want it all, and on and on it goes. With a provider welfare state more money simply means giving it more power to grow.

Feeding our welfare state beast is the root cause of jobs going overseas and the other stupid things that is happening today. Behind it all in truth is the liberals blind insane need to keep our provider welfare state beast as their Lord and Master. Whether we admit it or not we all are slaves to this beast. I rest my case, there is no reason to go on and on, if you don't get the point by now you never will.

Here is my blue print, Congress and the President must first, completely get rid of the minimum wage. Next, void all regulations on businesses, then add them back as needed. Next, establish government run commissaries, housing, and clinics and use token or script to prevent contaminating the nations free market economy. And finally, government must stop giving out free money and food stamps to anyone on an individual basis because that is what causes consume inflation and destroys the free market.

Also, all government spending and burdens should be limited to defense, treasure, state, interior, and only what the people can't do for themselves and collect taxes accordingly. In closing I suggest this blue print be taken seriously as a guide only. I am only trailblazing a path, with that I have done my duty.

I have no father control, may God bless this great nation. I am under no illusions, I know this blue print will be totally ignored; one reason is because U.S. Senators are no longer appointed by their states and the people are no longer the sole family providers. In reality whoever is the family providers actually rules and controls the country, it's just that simple in a free republic like ours. Cry me a river.

Now, in truth the welfare state has almost all of the real power. The states and the people can piss and moan and bitch all day long, but that's

about all in terms of making real changes. Instead of the United States senators being controlled by their state governor and congressmen they owe their real loyalty to special interest. And the people owe their real loyalty to who pays them, which is our welfare state with fewer and fewer exceptions.
SIRMANS LOG: 5 OCTOBER 2011, 1632 HOURS

9 OCTOBER 2011, 0844 HOURS, THIS INJECTION:
According to the U.S. constitution the military and protecting the nation is the first duty and priority of congress and the president. But, here we are today with a congress avoiding its duty by assigning it to a committee of six with OUR NATION SAVING military's neck on the chopping block.

In my one man's opinion that is a crying shame. My advice to congress is to take my advice and vote to eliminate the minimum wage right now, not tomorrow. That will get the ball rolling on saving our economy and the nation, God bless and keep a free America.

The constitution was originally designed for senators to represent the interest of their state government no one else's. That was the reason they were appointed instead of elected in the first place.

STIMULUS, STIMULUS, DUMB, DUMB, I THINK!
To me a stimulus package is like putting paper money down a rat hole. All it does is make a bad situation worse. When a nation is spending almost twice as much as it is taking in it is insane to think more spending is the answer, it is impossible to spend your way out of debt.

I truly understand how an economy works and to me the answer is very simple. The first truth is government spending is the problem and until that is recognized and admitted there is no saving the USA and global economy. What congress and the president needs to do first right now is recognize that this nations survival is at stake and act accordingly.

Instead of going on silly financial wild goose chases, void all regulations on businesses right now. Next, completely eliminate the minimum wage. Next, set up temporary emergency government run commissaries, government run housing in all these empty buildings, government run clinics, and use tokens or script for all who qualify for these government services.

Next, stop all government spending except for military and essential government only functions. I know to most this line of thinking will be seen as insane, but, I assure you the stimulus path will lead to guaranteed doom for the USA, or we end up as a debt slave owned and controlled by foreigners.

My way to salvation is only a

suggested path to take it doesn't have be word for word like I say but the path is a way out of no way, a word to the wise should be sufficient. God bless America.

PS: This path will set the USA economy free and guarantee without a shadow of doubt that entrepreneurs and the free market will save this great nation with freedom intact, nothing else can do that.

We must place all of our faith and trust in the proven ideology of the "Free market place at work.
SIRMANS LOG: 1 SEPTEMBER 2011, 0846 HOURS

IS HURRICANES THE WRATH OF AN ANGRY GOD?
The ancients certainly thought so and came up with human sacrifices and all kinds of appeasements. Believe it or not, however, excluding the sacrifices there are still some that fall prey to that type of thinking.

Myself, to that type of thinking I say poppycock, hogwash, bullcrap, or some other tits on a boar hog like metaphor. It is all nonsense, what goes around comes around and that includes the works of Mother Nature. It also includes the working of every economy, too.

Every economy has a boon and bust cycle and sooner or later the bust cycle is going to come back around no matter how much scheming and fine tuning the egg heads does. That is just a fact of life.

So, when we become dumb and stupid and let the welfare state replace and destroy our bread and butter nuclear and extended family system that leaves us up S... Creek without a paddle.

Today when most people first read my writing they think I must be some kind of extreme right wing kook or loon that is out of touch. What they don't realize is one hundred years or so ago 95 percent of Americans though as I do.

The validity of a strong nuclear and extended family system with good morals and values haven't changed in five thousand years, it is we who have changed for the worst as a people since the "New deal" birthed our welfare state.

When the wood chopper gave up on trying to splitting a mighty oak block before walking away he decided to knee down and take a closer look. And sure enough he could barely see it but there was a tiny beginning split. He realized all of his long hard effort had not been totally wasted.

I feel the same as the great wood chopper, except after all these years of my writing effort I still can't see any reward, I wish I could just quit and walk away and never look back, but, I know I must carry on as long as any life left in me. I guess if I can enlighten just one person it will have been worth it.

SIRMANS LOG: 30 AUGUST 2011, 1135 HOURS.

GOD BLESS OUR FEDERAL RESERVE! This idea of getting rid of the Federal Reserve is just plain dumb and stupid. That is like saying get rid of the government. You can't have an organized society without government.

There must be a government to protect and safeguard the whole society. However, what I am against is a welfare state type of government, which I believe is unconstitutional. Without government means anarchy with every man for himself.

The same thing applies to the economy; there must be some type of organized money system. Otherwise, you are left with only trade and bartering to survive. These people talking about getting rid of the Federal Reserve are just plain ignorant, it is the best organized money system known to man.

What type of currency to use is left up to congress and the president? Maybe it's time congress and the president consider getting back to a genuine physical currency with its value in the currency itself. But, to seriously consider getting rid of the Federal Reserve is shallow and short sighted.

What are you going to replace it with, a feudal system with Lords and castles, I think not. Right or wrong that is my one man's opinion.
SIRMANS LOG: 21 AUGUST 2011, 0730 HOURS

FOOD STAMP'S DESTRUCTIVE POWER! I place food stamps as the third most destructive force behind the "New deal" and the minimum wage to a genuine free market place economy.

Number one is the "New deal" when it started giving free unearned money to the poor. Sure, the poor must be helped as a last resort and not allowed to starve. But, if the free market place is to survive the government must never give out free unearned money to anyone.

The only way the government can help the poor and disadvantage without destroying the free market place is by temporary establishing government run commissaries, housing, and clinics. And even that should be done only as a last resort after the extended family, the church, the community, and all else has failed.

Otherwise a survival need for the nuclear and extended family will be replaced by government and in time the nuclear family will cease to exist. The reason why that will in time kill every economy is because there are only two players in an economy; they are a seller and a buyer or merchant and consumer.

The government is only a necessary parasite needed to protect the whole society. Government has the power and the big guns and many times takes over and run the whole show, but only a free market place economy can feed its entire population.

In a free country if government would just stay with collecting taxes, protecting the country, and doing only what the people can't do for themselves the economy would police itself and produce far more than the population could use.

Mother Nature's supreme law of "Natural selection" would maintain a natural balance between the buyers and sellers and purge out inefficiency, moral decay and other anti-survival forces. But, when government takes its tax money and gives out on an individual basis free unearned money and food stamps to the poor that creates enough people with the money to keep higher and higher priced merchants in business.

Then the government raises the taxes on the higher and higher priced merchants and the merchants passes their extra cost on to the public in a never ending inflationary spiral. After the "New deal" and the government started giving out free unearned money on an individual basis that ignited inflation but by then government had tasted the God like power of being a super provider.

Then the die was cast and I don't believe big government ever intend to give up one inch of its cradle to grave God like great white father provider role come hell or high waters. When it comes to money it is not the amount that truly matters it is the buying power that really counts.

Once inflation kicks in higher taxes on merchants only means higher prices passed on to the public. I didn't research when the minimum wage was started but at some point government decided the minimum was a good idea, I totally disagree.

All the minimum wage does is remove the safety valve from a free market place economy, it is then like a vehicle with no reverse or a hot water heater with no pop off valve. Folks, now don't get me all twisted I know the things I criticize was genuine intended to help the poor and to a lesser extent get politicians elected.

I know food stamps was meant to be a good thing but just like free unearned cash it is deadly destructive to a free market place economy when given out on an individual basis.

With government not giving out free money to the poor It is impossible for most merchants to charge more than the poor can pay and stay in business because there is never enough rich to keep commerce flowing. When government is not involved in the free market place that will keep the cost of living down to where the people can pay their on food and doctor bills.

When government do help the poor and disadvantage by establishing government run commissaries, housing, and clinics it should always use tokens or scripts. That will make

sure government spending is kept separate and not contaminate the nation's economy in any way.
SIRMANS LOG: 17 AUGUST 2011, 1245 HOURS.

LAST CALL TO ELIMINATE THE MINIMUM WAGE!
The egg heads, the ruling class, and the elites all think I'm some kind of nut case that few knows about and I should be ignored out of existence, wrong.

When I keep harping on completely eliminating the minimum wage they think I'm a fool and don't know what I am talking about, wrong.
Eliminating the minimum wage is the only thing that is going to save western civilization by starving the welfare state beast out of its all powerful super provider role.

That and that alone can set the free market place free to save western civilization. Nothing else can do it. That act alone will permit the nuclear and extended family system to rebound along with good moral and plenty of emergency life sustaining bartering capacity. Otherwise, if we fail to eliminate the minimum wage western civilization is done.

It will very soon have zero chance of surviving. The reason is Mother Nature herself is going to use its supreme law of "Natural selection" to reset western civilization back to zero, in other words the Stone Age.

The welfare state has destroyed 90 percent of the foundation that holds every society together. And without the elimination of the minimum wage the welfare state will complete the job with 100 percent destruction. I'm talking about a 100 percent destruction of the nuclear and extended family system.

As to good ethics and morals, right now we have men marring men and women marring women and before long good ethics and morals will be something found only in the history

books. And the old standby of
having adequate emergency backup
bartering capacity in case the
economy fails, meaning many, many
small farmers and home gardeners,
they are now like so many, sucking on
the welfare state provider tit.

Just in case anyone is thinking that if
things get out of hand martial law
will be used to demand order by force,
could be in for a rude awakening.
At this point western civilization
without eliminating the minimum wage
soon won't have any foundation left to
support civilization or an
organized society.

That being the case no amount of
authority can prevent total chaos back
to the Stone Age. Only the elimination
of the minimum wage can save
what little that is left of a foundation to
survive on and reverse course
before going over the cliff and taking
western civilization with it.

Of course, I know I will be ignored
more than ever but I believe my

great supernatural wisdom is God given. Go ahead a laugh and dismiss me as a bigger nut than ever, but, one thing is for sure "We all dance to the tune of a distance drummer." Glory be to God.

The real secret is, life is all about maintaining a balance, and I know most of my views are too one sided and to the extreme, but only drastic thinking and actions at this late stage can create a middle balance.

Once the minimum wage is eliminated the next step is the government must never give out free money to help anyone on an individual basis. To help the poor, needy or anyone the government must establish temporary commissaries, housing, and clinics and use tokens or script for those that qualify.

That will prevent government spending from igniting inflation and destroying the free marking place like what is killing today's economy. I assure you sooner or later some

nation is going to see the light and grab my no minimum wage lifeline wisdom, not every one is going to play Russian roulette with their nations' survival.
SIRMANS LOG: 07 AUGUST 2011, 0011 HOURS

"OOPS! THERE IT IS!"
Like I've said before, the liberals will see you in hell before they will cut spending and stop the growth of government. For whatever reasons, those pushing for the collapse of the USA and global economies, it may be all down hill from here.

I knew it, I knew it, the conservatives and others would not be able to withstand the pressure, now I guarantee you taxes are going to be raised on the fewer and fewer businesses left standing. Lord knows I hope I'm wrong on this, but I'm afraid this may be the final nail in the coffin before the sunsets of the USA and global economies.

Like a broken record I'm still at it on pleading for the eliminating of the minimum wage. I yell to the world this welfare state beast is out of control and is just too powerful and mighty. But like David with his stone and sling shot I promise you, the elimination of the "Minimum wage will bring this beast to its knees and put the people back in control over their government.

Nothing else is going to break its death grip on the USA and global economies. The dam is about to burst, and once the dominos start falling no one knows where it's going to end, it may be back to the Stone Age, only God knows, God save America, Amen.
SIRMANS LOG: 02 AUGUST 2011, 1455 HOURS

THE FORGOTTEN, ONLY GUARANTEED PENSION!
What this entitlement generation has forgotten or don't even know is for over 5000 years your only survival

pension was your children.

Until around eighty years ago when the "New deal" and this monster size welfare state came about the nuclear and extended family system allowed civilization to exist for over 5000 years. It is not a perfect system but no society have ever survived and existed without it in the history of man kind.

In the USA except for maybe a few veterans almost no one was on the government dole before the "New deal" came along. Sure, in the beginning social security was a good thing for the elderly and the severely disadvantaged, but now every body and his brother is on it.

Those that put all of their faith in government don't know history, there has never been a government that didn't go broke at some point. To let this big government welfare state kill the nuclear family system by taking away it survival need like what is happening is not only dumb and stupid it is sheer madness.

Never put all of your survival eggs in one basket, especially a tax hungry out of control welfare state beast. The biggest problem now is the welfare state has produced so many dependents so long that nearly 40 percent of the population has no clue as how to survive using self-initiative.

I wish somebody would please show me how in the hell you are going to pay your way out of debt by going deeper into debt, like the liberals are trying to do.
SIRMANS LOG: 30 JULY 2011, 2025 HOURS.

MASS ECONOMIC IGNORANCE!
About 95 percent of the American people's knowledge of how an economy truly works can be compared to a little kid that believes grits and eggs come only from the grocery store.

Even most economist has bought into this liberal garbage claptrap entitlement mentality that started with the "New deal." But, I'm here to tell you there are no free rides in life somebody always pays.

All wealth originates from some type of trade or business transaction by the private sector, period. No wealth originates from government it is always taken from somebody or somewhere. The first rule in economic is "You can't get blood out of a turnip."

You can't eat money and if there are not enough people producing food there is going to be starvation no matter who the liberals blame. When a nation prevents the private sector from making a profit it cuts its own throat that is biting the hand that feeds it.

Only a free market place nation can create wealth and feed its entire people, all other economic systems leads to mass starvation, that is the history, you can look it up. But, when

have a liberal ever had common sense, very seldom in my view.
SIRMANS LOG: 29 JULY 2011, 0859 HOURS

WELFARE STATE DEATH GRIP MUST BE BROKEN!
As I set back and watch all of the ado going on about raising the debt ceiling I just take the whole thing with a grain of salt. In the grand scheme of things it really doesn't matter if they raise it or not because all that is doing is buying just a wee little more time.

Either way it is not going to stop the welfare state from killing off both the USA and global economies. As a supposition example, if miraculous all of the USA's debt and financial problems were solved today, we as a nation will still be doomed.

The reason is money and lack of jobs are direct and obvious, but the real things that hold every society together is not so obvious and have rotted away to the very core because of the welfare state. Number one, the base and foundation for all human survival are the nuclear and extended family system.

Nothing can exist and be strong without a survival need, and the welfare state has took away that need for the strong nuclear family and left this great nation with no means to survive when the going get rough, and believe me tough times is just over the horizon. And the other two critical survival means of good morals and adequate emergency backup bartering capacity are practical nonexistence.

I know no one want to hear it, but I repeat again and again that the only thing that is going to save the USA and western civilization is the complete elimination of the minimum wage as a start. Nothing else can break the death grip the welfare state have on this nation's economic throat; otherwise the welfare state is going to finish off the kill.
SIRMANS LOG: 23 JULY 2011, 0005

HOURS

INFLATION'S BIGGEST MYTH AND MISCONCEPTION!
The biggest misconception about inflation is that the mass printing of money by government is the cause of inflation, wrong. Government can print all of the money it wants to and that alone will not ignite the cost of living consumer inflation.

So, OK, the government prints up all of this worthless money? But, in order to ignite inflation it has to get that money to enough people on an individual basis to corrupt the natural balance between the merchant and the consumer. Handing out free unearned money on an individual basis that and that alone is the cause of the cost of living consumer inflation.

That is why I keep screaming so loud that government should never give out free unearned money on an individual basis. Sure, as a last resort

www.ingramcontent.com/pod-product-compliance
Lightning Source LLC
Chambersburg PA
CBHW061505180526
45171CB00001B/49